FOLLOWING JESUS into college and beyond

Jeff Baxter

ZONDERVAN®

ZONDERVAN.com/
AUTHORTRACKER
follow your favorite authors

ZONDERVAN®

Following Jesus into College and Beyond
Copyright © 2009 by Jeff Baxter

Requests for information should be addressed to:

Zondervan, *Grand Rapids, Michigan* 49530

ISBN 978-0-310-28263-1

Cover design by Mark Novelli, IMAGO MEDIA
Interior design by SharpSeven Design and David Conn

Printed in the United States of America

09 10 11 12 13 14 • 23 22 21 20 19 18 17 16 15 14 13 12 11 10 9 8 7 6 5 4 3 2 1

This book is dedicated to those closest to my heart:

Laurie, Lillian, Levi, and Lara.

I love you.

FOREWORD

BY CHAP CLARK

This is a good book. But more than that, it's a really important book. If you're preparing for college or just beginning your college years, I hope you'll make a plan not only to read this book, but to go through it slowly and carefully—taking notes and talking about it with those who know and love you.

Do you have any idea how many high school disciples, and I mean the ones most people consider "real Christians"—those who take Jesus seriously, who sincerely intend to follow him for the rest of their lives, and who have made sacrificial choices in the face of strong opposition because of their faith—end up feeling, in the few months or years after high school, that they've let their faith slip into the background of their lives, or simply blown it off altogether? There's disagreement over exact figures, but everybody agrees the number is huge. The question is: As you make the transition into college and beyond, how will you not only keep your faith but flourish as a powerful, committed, vibrant follower of Jesus? That's what this book is all about.

Jeff Baxter wrote this book to help you grab hold of all that God has for you. *Following Jesus into College and Beyond* is an honest, clear, and practical guide that will give you the chance to really soar as you explore Christ's unique calling for you. If you sincerely go after what's here, you will be changed, for three reasons:

Jeff gets it. He has spent many years moving in and around the lives of high school and college students. He has spent lots of time (and money) to get a top-level education that helps him understand how growing up today is different than it was even ten years ago. And Jeff has dedicated himself to pursuing Christ with everything he's got—and even though he's far from perfect (I know him pretty well), he knows the Christian life that usually gets talked about can be far different from how it works out in real life. Jeff gets it, and he cares. You are safe and respected in his hands.

Most of what's in this book will probably be new to you, and likely to your parents, friends, and even your youth leader—but you need to know it. As you read this book, be sure to take notes, pray, and open yourself up to others who can walk with you through the issues Jeff highlights. The new insights he shares will give you a deeper awareness of who you are, what trips you up and why, and where you're going as the person God has created and called. This is *not* a "textbook," it is a friend and a guide that can help you see more clearly where you are headed and where your steps are landing along the way.

If you will read carefully, and listen carefully to God through the Scriptures, by his Spirit, and in the words of others, you will discover that the gospel is more about the place God is taking you than the place you have been. The more you can cultivate a forward-leaning trust in Jesus, especially compared with a faith that worries or compromises or is shackled by the past, the more you will see and experience the power of God working in your life.

You see, our lives and our growth are not for us, they are for our Lord. Life comes down to a single adventure: Following God's lead as he brings in his kingdom, and living out this quest alongside all who have heard and responded to his call. As you grow into the man or woman God has created and bought to new life through his Spirit, this book will be an important friend along the way.

Chap Clark, PhD
Professor of Youth, Family, and Culture
Fuller Theological Seminary

ACKNOWLEDGMENTS
(FOR THE PEOPLE WHO MADE THIS THING HAPPEN)

Jesus Christ:
...for being the same yesterday, today, and forever.

Laurie:
...for walking through this life with me.

Lillian, Levi, and Lara:
...for giving me grace as I live this stuff out in front of you.

Mom and Dad:
...for introducing me to Jesus and drilling me on spelling words.

My Extended Family:
...for chuckling at my dry humor.

Chap Clark:
...for further opening the door to understanding the adolescent world.

Jay Howver:
...for asking me to take a crack at writing this book.

Doug, Erin, and the Rest of the YS/Zondervan Team:
...for your patience and help in making this book faithful.

Columbia International University Professors:
...for teaching and modeling a passion for Scripture.

High School and College Students and Twentysomethings across the Nation:
...for providing the meaty quotes throughout this book.

Foothills Bible Church:
...for allowing me to partner with you to reach the next generation.

My Prayer Partners:
...for going to the One who can do more than we can ask or imagine.

INTRODUCTION
(OR THE PART MOST OF US DON'T READ, BUT REALLY SHOULD)

I'm excited to get out into the real world and become who God intends me to be, but I'm extremely nervous. What if I fail? How will I know if I'm doing what I should? I pray about my future a lot, that God will help me to make the right decisions. —Jaclyn, 17

Hi, I'm Jeff—the guy who wrote this book. I'm thrilled you're reading it, because I believe it has the potential to alter your life for good.

Following Jesus into College and Beyond is written for high school students and recent graduates who are making the transition from life as a high school student to life in the real world. Whether your next step is college, a job, or something else, my goal is to help you ask the right questions and really think about what it means to follow Jesus for the long haul. It's my hope this book will also be helpful to parents, youth pastors, teachers, and others who seek to partner with students as they make the all-important transition from high school to life after graduation.

I probably don't need to tell you the life of the average high school student has changed dramatically over the past decade or two. We adults love to say, "When I was in high school, I used to...." Doesn't it drive you crazy when you hear that? Well, times have changed too much for this one-liner. With all of the challenges and potential temptations connected with MySpace, Facebook, Internet porn, advertisements, date rape, terrorism, depression, cutting, all sorts of pressures and stresses—it's a brand-new world out there. Did I mention it's stressful? I know you understand this, so I'm not going to beat around the bush. I'm not all that old, but I'm very aware the pressures you face are much different than the ones I faced when I was in high school. I think it's much more difficult to negotiate the treacherous waters of your world.

> *You're about to begin a new chapter of your life; a clean, new page. Allow God to pen the words of this chapter into a beautiful masterpiece of worship.*
> *—Ryan, 24*

This book is all about helping you stay afloat in those waters. It's filled with quotes from other teenagers just like you who are preparing to head out the high school doors into the world, as well as advice from college students and other twentysomethings who've been through the transitional years. These quotes are taken from surveys I sent out to hundreds of high school and college students. I'll draw from my years in ministry inside and outside the local church, and do my best to provide you with insights I've gathered as an adult who's a student of Jesus, culture, teenagers, college students, and twentysomethings.

I hope you'll think of this book as a buffet. I've tried to set a table with a wide variety of foods that can nourish your soul. So with help from our heavenly Father, come to the book-buffet. Take whatever you like—maybe eat dessert first! Leave what's not helpful, but eat till your heart's content. My prayer is that the truths in this book will help you make a smooth transition into college and beyond.

Welcome to the Customize-Everything World

Have you noticed you can customize just about everything these days? Think about it: Cars have custom designs from the front bumper to the muffler. (And that's just the outside of the car!) If you have a cell phone (and if you don't, you need one before you leave for college), you know you can choose your own skin, ringtone, and display, morphing it into personalized eye candy. Your computer's desktop is arranged just the way you like it. You can customize your MySpace or Facebook page until it stands out from that of your friends.

And how about coffee? I love coffee. I remember when the only choice to make when ordering was whether to add sugar or cream; but that's not how it goes today. Now the jingle goes something like this: "I'll take a grande, low-fat, iced carmel macchiato with extra carmel drizzle." (Okay, maybe forget the low-fat part.) I was so proud the last time I ordered a latte because all the boxes on the side of the cup were checked. They even took my name and wrote it on the cup. It was customized, baby!

> *I'm really excited for everything—college, family, and ministry— and yet sometimes I get caught up in thinking I can't be used now while I'm still in high school. But I can. I don't have to wait for college to start looking for opportunities to serve others. —Haylee, 15*

But what about your life? Can we customize our lives? As you make this transition from high school to life after high school—which might mean college, work, or both—you have a great opportunity to customize your life, to make it your own. For many of you this is as exciting as it comes. You've been waiting and longing for years to enter the "real world." Others of you may find it mostly terrifying—all the responsibilities that come with the adult world might have you hiding in your closest while reading this book.

Most likely it's a combination of feelings, and it changes depending on the day. Like a blossoming baby bird, you excitedly think you're ready to fly the coop. So you jump out of the nest and attempt to fly only to discover your feathers haven't fully developed yet. Gravity takes over, and down you go. Needless to say this brings stressful times and deep wounds. I hope this book will help you grow your feathers long and strong so you can steadily soar at 10,000 feet (and avoid most of the bumps and bruises along the way)!

The Interruption

Have you ever been interrupted right in the middle of something? Maybe you were doing some homework and your little sister came walking into your room. Or maybe you're a songwriter, and you were on a roll when your best friend called. If you like puzzles (like my family does), you might not like to be interrupted.

Interruptions are distracting. They slow things down. Once, my oldest sister interrupted my freshman basketball team's practice. It was right around my birthday (December 10), and she was home from college. She decided to show up dressed as Mrs. Claus, and she brought birthday cupcakes. When she walked in the gym, everyone stopped what they were doing. The varsity players, junior-varsity players, freshman players—they all stopped, held their basketballs, and waited to see who Mrs. Claus intended to visit. She waltzed over and gave the cupcakes to me. I love my sister, but at the time her impromptu celebration was an interruption to my free-throw practice—and a new addition to my list of top-ten-most-embarrassing moments.

Your transition into adulthood might seem like one great big interruption. It's distracting, upsetting, out-of-place, exciting, and nerve-racking all at the same time. As one twentysomething explained, "Young adults are in the middle: not married, not old enough, not in high school. We're in this 'ugh' stage." I'll bet you want to be a full-fledged adult so badly you could scream. You're tired of people treating you like a child. But this phase of life you're going through is distinct, unique, and normal. Lots of changes are happening, and many people have mixed feelings about these changes.

Take a look at what some high school students had to say about the transition to college and beyond. (You'll find quotes from other students scattered throughout this book.) See if there are any you can identify with:

> *I'm more than ready to leave the high school scene, to enter the real world and meet people who are a little more focused and a little more spiritually and emotionally mature. I'm not at all nervous because I know God will take care of me, but I'm really ready to move on to better things. —Shae, 18*

> *I'm very nervous because I have no clue what I will do after high school. I know I shouldn't be nervous because God holds my life in his hands and has a plan for me. —Brooke, 17*

> *I have mixed emotions about becoming an adult. I'm excited to see what God brings into my life, but very nervous because I don't really know what's going to happen. It's a great adventure. —Annabel, 15*

As you look toward the future, maybe you feel pure excitement. Or maybe you feel pure terror. Perhaps you connect with the mixture of nervousness and excitement Annabel describes. I hope this book will help calm your nerves and energize your spirit as you head into this great adventure of following Jesus.

When Does Your Real World Begin?

In the United States you're legally considered an adult on the day you turn 18. Once you're 18 a variety of privileges and responsibilities are yours: You can vote, own property, buy tobacco, marry without parental consent, be tried as an adult if you commit a crime, and even buy things from infomercials on late-night TV. So congratulations: If you're 18 or older, society says you're an adult. But is this really what adulthood is all about?

My hunch? You already know there's more to being an adult than simply reaching a particular birthday. There are more questions to answer, more things to figure out if you're really going to be an adult, especially a mature adult who follows Jesus.

I'm writing this book with the prayer that it'll help you figure out how to become an adult fully mature in Jesus. You don't become one automatically when you turn 18; you become one when you've fully engaged the journey toward maturity. Sooner or later everyone will become an adult. I want to help you get there before you're 40 years old! Trust me, I know some 40-year-olds who haven't made it yet! (I'm sure you know some, too.)

In this book we'll explore three critical themes of what it means for you to follow Jesus into college and beyond.

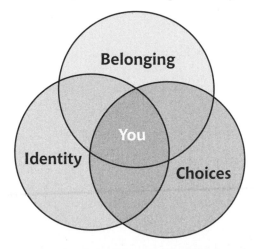

In each of these areas, we'll tackle questions about becoming a follower of Christ. Deep down you're longing to answer these questions for yourself. This is a natural process during the transition from adolescence to adulthood.

> **ONE** – Identity: Who am I? Who am I suppose to be, and what do I know to be true? Can I doubt sometimes?

> **TWO** – Choices: Do my decisions really matter? How much control of my life do I have? How do I handle the new responsibilities coming my way as an adult? How will I handle college? Is it okay if I'm stressed out?

> **THREE** – Belonging: Where do I fit? What does this world have for me? What does God have for me? Where do family, friends, and dating fit? How important is it for me to connect to the local church?

My guess is you're already thinking about these questions and searching for your own answers. I look forward to helping you consider who you are, why your choices matter, and what it means to belong to the family of God.

I have no idea what I want to do with my life, so I'm nervous about making the wrong decisions and messing up my future.
—Justine, 17

The Goal of This Book

As you work through this book (but more importantly as you work through this transition from adolescence to adulthood), I want to help you grow. So maybe I should let you know right from the start: I'm not a fabulous gardener. I wish I had a green thumb, but I don't. But I do know a little about planting things. My family has done our share of landscaping homes over the years. I know you need the right things for plants and trees to grow. I know certain plants need to be in the shade and others need more sunlight. I know some plants need more water and others hardly need any water at all.

But most of all I know it's God who does the growing. Sometimes I've thought I was the one who did the growing, but I understand my two poplar trees won't grow without God orchestrating the process.

There are images of gardens and growth throughout the Bible. Scripture begins with Adam and Eve. They walked in the Garden of Eden in great fellowship with God until they made a decision to disobey God and eat fruit from the forbidden tree (Genesis 2-3). Jesus has an interesting connection to gardens, too. He visited gardens throughout his life to pray. In fact, just hours before he died on the cross, he prayed in a garden asking his heavenly Father to sustain him (Matthew 26:36-46; Mark 14:32-42; and Luke 22:40-46).

God cares a great deal about healthy growth. He wants you to grow in maturity, faith, obedience, health, wisdom, strength, and all other good things! So I'll play the part of the gardener by setting you up for growth with the right themes and questions. Your responsibility will be to partner with God in the process. Plant yourself in the right environment to be watered, fertilized, sunned, nurtured, and loved so you have the best shot at growing into a mature follower of Jesus. You can't always determine your environment, but as much as it depends on you, situate yourself so you can grow closer to Jesus as you make this transition. Helping you do that is the goal of this book.

> I'm not really nervous, but I don't want to graduate and leave. I love high school. It has been an awesome experience that I don't want to end. —Kurt, 17

You can use this book several different ways. You can read it straight through. If you're a high school student, not everything will make sense yet. Don't worry; keep pressing on. Take the book with you as you journey to and through college. As different difficulties and situations arise, read it again. You can also use this book as a reference guide. Be sure to underline, circle, and highlight relevant passages. (You can write in the margins, too! I won't tell.)

You can also share this book with your friends. Following Jesus is meant to be done in community, not solitude. You can use the questions at the end of each chapter to start discussions with your Jesus-following friends as well as friends who don't know Jesus yet. Wrestle with the ideas and questions together. You might not agree with me at certain times—that's okay. Keep wrestling and pursuing Jesus as you make your transition into the real world. Aim for maturity, and God will help you get there.

Walking with Jesus isn't always easy, but you'll find the path brings growth, maturity, and life at its best. I'm so glad you've decided to join me on this journey!

PART ONE:

IDENTITY – Who Am I?

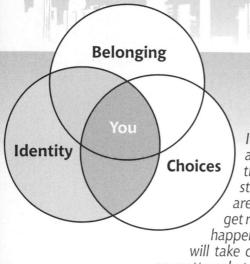

I'm very excited about becoming an adult, and I look forward to the rest of my life with college and starting a family some day. There are some days I think about it, and I get really nervous. But I know whatever happens in my life is for a reason. God will take care of me and be there with me no matter what. —Brittney, 17

The question, "Who am I?" is probably driving you crazy by now. In the back of your mind, or deep down in the core of your heart, you're probably still wondering what the answer is to this all-important question. When you get up in the morning, look in the mirror, get ready for school, eat breakfast, brush your teeth (after you eat breakfast, I hope), drive to school, walk the halls, sit in class, go to work, and face every social situation you can think of, I bet this question pumps through your veins. Am I right? Think about it!

Whether you're already out of high school or moving closer and closer to graduation, you may feel like you should have it figured out by now. But the question remains: "Who am I really?" To make things worse, everyone else seems to know you better than you know yourself. They say, "That's not like you," and you think, How do you know what's like me? How do you know who I am?

The world may say your job, upbringing, family, or money defines you, but God says it's your relationship with him that truly defines you. (See Psalm 139:15-16.) As you move through the next stages of your life, you'll develop a better understanding of who you are. As you become more independent of your parents upon leaving high school, I hope you become more interdependent on God and a community of Jesus-followers in the context of a local church.

Discovering who you are is a bit like dancing. In this section, we'll explore some of the more challenging steps in that dance by looking at your story in Scripture, your belief in Jesus, your God-given design, and the role of doubts. Don't worry if you're not a good dancer. (I know I'm not!) This section will help you learn some of the basics. Before you know it, you'll be dancing like a pro.

CHAPTER I

SCRIPTURE: YOUR IDENTITY IN GOD'S STORY

God is the Word and the Word is God. If I want to be closer to him, I have to listen to what He's telling me. No relationship has ever worked when one person spoke and the other always chose not to listen, so how can my relationship with God work if I choose not to listen to him?—Shae, 18

A Good Narrative

We're all drawn to a good story, aren't we? Stories are fun. But what is it about a story that brings us in, grabs hold of us, and doesn't let go until there's some sort of resolution?

My uncle is a master storyteller. As long as I can remember, Uncle Deane has told stories and jokes in dramatic fashion. He draws you in with his gestures and engages you with his theatrics and vocal inflections. The golf course is one of his favorite places to tell stories. We could probably finish a round of golf a few hours earlier if it weren't for his tales, but they're worth every minute.

In *The Living Reminder,* author Henri Nouwen talks about the power of stories:

> We can dwell in a story, walk around, and find our own place. The story confronts but does not oppress; the story inspires but does not manipulate. The story invites us to an encounter, a dialog, a mutual sharing. A story that guides is a story that opens a door and offers space in which to search and boundaries to help us find what we seek.

Stories connect with the deepest longings inside us—and I think that's because each of our lives is its own story. Our individual stories are all intimately connected. Our lives come together to form a divine tapestry—a single, great, big, human story.

When interviewing for various jobs, I've often been asked some form of the question, "What's your story?" Those interviewers wanted to know where I came from and what makes me tick. They wanted to know what was important to me and how my passions, gifts, and abilities drove me to action. Similarly, in the college and post-college ministries I've led, we ask the attendees to share their stories every week—not just their testimonies about when they came to know Jesus, but their current stories. We want to know what they're learning about life and God. We're interested in authentic connection. We long to know—really know—one another. By sharing stories, our community members learn what drives one another, what we're currently learning, and what our common struggles are. This is inspiring. This is divine tapestry.

So what's your story? Spend some time right now thinking about your past. Consider the great joys of your life as well as the hard times God has led you through. If you know Jesus, think of how you came to know him. Maybe you remember the exact point in time and could mark a date on the calendar. Or maybe you just remember how old you were when you surrendered to him. Whatever the case, God directed you to this point. Celebrate his guiding grace as we begin to think about how all of our stories connect.

Our stories connect to one another's, but they also connect to the larger story of God's work in our world. It's a grand narrative. God made humanity because God loves to tell stories. The psalmist in the Old Testament says:

> You created my inmost being; you knit me together in my mother's womb. I praise you because I am fearfully and wonderfully made; your works are wonderful. I know that full well. My frame was not hidden from you when I was made in the secret place. When I was woven together in the depths of the earth, your eyes saw my unfolded body. All the days ordained for me were written in your book before one of them came to be. (Psalm 139:13-16)

Your story is connected to something greater.

Dog Bones

Have you ever watched a dog with a bone? My dog, Mocha, loves bones. Each bone is her prize, and she protects it at all costs. She growls playfully—a low rumble expressing her delight. When she's done gnawing on a bone, she licks her chops and paws. And bones aren't her only joy: She's been known to put her front paws on the counter, snatch a loaf of bread, and devour it. One time we thought she'd eaten a whole bag of bagels, only to discover she'd buried them in our couches and chairs for later!

As I was studying Scripture one day, I found a verse that compares God to "a great lion" growling over its prey (Isaiah 31:4). I thought of Mocha growling over her bone. This is when it gets really fun. The Hebrew word for growl is *hagah*. Say it out loud: *Hagah*. It's a fun word that can also mean *to meditate*. So Mocha—with these low growls of enjoyment and playful delight over her bone—is meditating over her prize.

Scripture uses *hagah* in other ways, too. The very first Psalm says our delight should be "in the law of the Lord—meditate on it day and night" (Psalm 1:1-2). The psalmist says he thinks about God on his bed at night. He dwells on God (Psalm 63:6). The word *hagah* was used by the Jews for reading, studying, meditating, and apparently for growling. With *hagah* we use our teeth, tongue, taste buds, stomach, and intestines for chewing, swallowing, and digesting. With *hagah* we understand God is good: "Taste and see that the Lord is good" (Psalm 34:8).

> *I study Scripture every night: sometimes for hours, sometimes just a page before I fall asleep. Sometimes it's monotonous, but often times God shows me some gem I'd never seen or realized before and it changes my life. Without these insights, I'd be lost. —David, 18*

What happens as we truly mediate on the stories of Scripture? We find them to be alive with meaning for us today. We discover more and more ways in which the pieces of *our* stories intersect with God's story. This is a *hagah* moment.[1]

Directional Dysfunction

I have a problem, and I'm willing to admit it: I'm terrible with directions. If there is a disease characterized by frequent disorientation, I'm pretty sure I've got it. As a matter of fact, I think I'll start a recovery group called A.D.D. (not that kind, although I might have that, too)—All-Direction Dysfunctional.

How are you with directions? How's your internal compass? Have you ever been to a new place and didn't have a clue where anything was?

When my wife, Laurie, and I moved to Littleton, Colorado, we didn't know where anything was located. We didn't know street names. We didn't know where anyone lived. We didn't know where

---

1 Eugene Peterson inspired my study of the Hebrew word *hagah* in his book *Eat This Book* (Eerdmans, 2006).

our church was in relation to everywhere else. We couldn't find a Wal-Mart or a Target. We didn't know how to find the zoo, where to get an oil change, or where to find a dentist or hospital. And most critically, we couldn't find the nearest Starbucks or the Barnes and Noble! Thank goodness for those mountains in the west—at least I knew where they were (until it got dark)!

So what do you think we did to learn where things were located in Littleton? Do you think we sat down with a map and memorized where every street was? That would never work for me. We learned as we lived. We kept our eyes open. We asked questions. We looked at MapQuest (a lot). We went for drives to look around, especially for a home. When we visited a new location, we paid attention. We started to observe the same places, and eventually we found Starbucks, Target, and the nearest gas station. We discovered where people lived in relation to one another. Before long, we had a pretty good grasp of where to go and how to get there.

> *The Bible is the record of what God said and did in history, so it has to be a priority for us to study it and be familiar with it. It's through the Bible we see how Jesus treated people, showed love, and approached the world. Without it, we're not going to be able to grow much at all.*
> *—Adam, 23*

When it comes to studying Scripture, many of us feel the same way. We feel lost. We know a few landmark stories, but have no idea how all of these little stories fit into the larger, God-sized story. And we don't know how our own personal stories are a part of God's story. As we study Scripture, we need to discover as we go.

A friend of mine once said, "You can't steer a parked car." You won't learn how your story fits with God's story unless you open Scripture and start reading. As you travel further into Scripture, you'll discover connections. You'll begin to remember other, similar places. You'll begin to think to yourself, *Oh, I get it. The sacrifices they talk about in the Old Testament are connected to Jesus being the last and most important sacrifice for me.* The stories will begin to connect—with each other and with your life.

As you read the stories of Scripture, try to experience them in your imagination. Try to picture yourself visiting the Sea of Galilee and listening to Jesus teach. What would the water look like as it laps against the skyline? What does Jesus' voice sound like? How does the sand feel between your toes? As you travel through the Scriptures, look for landmarks—key people, places, and events. These landmarks can help guide you to the main story just as the picture on a puzzle box helps you see where the pieces fit. You might find it helpful to read summaries of various books of the Bible as a way of grasping the bigger story. Or you may want to slow down and learn one location at a time by focusing on a particular character, theme, or book within Scripture. Glimpsing the big picture, then slowing down to enjoy the view, is important.

> I need Scripture! It has become my addiction. I don't even think I do it right, but God is teaching me every day.
> —Annie, 29

Glancers and Gazers

A few summers ago I led a team of high school students on a two-week leadership-experience trip in Europe. On the last day we hung out in Paris. (It was awesome!) Of course a few of us went to the Louvre, the famous museum that houses the *Mona Lisa* and many other well-known paintings.

The Louvre is made up of eight departments that display 35,000 works in 60,000 square meters of exhibition space. It's huge. After an hour or two of looking around, I needed a break. I did what many people do during a break: I people-watched.

As I observed thousands of people coming and going, I noticed two types: glancers and gazers. The glancers did their best to look at every piece of art in the Louvre within a few hours. That would be impossible—even if you looked at each piece of art for just a minute, you'd need three weeks to see them all. But these glancers did their best to see everything and never spent too much time on any one piece of art.

On the other hand there were the gazers. These folks were students of history, art, and culture. They'd stop at one painting, look at it from every angle, notice the fine details, take pictures, and write notes in their journals. A gazer might spend an hour in front of a single piece of art before moving on.

In the same way, I've noticed two types of Scripture students. There are glancers who quickly read but don't take the time to understand how all the stories fit together. They seem primarily focused on "getting it done." The gazers seem to take their time. They read and study, seeking to understand how God's story intersects with our stories. Gazers long to fall more deeply in love with God.

There's a big difference between reading and studying Scripture. Thomas à Kempis once said, "Do not read the Scriptures to satisfy curiosity or to pass the time, but study such things as to move your heart to devotion." Let the greater story work on you.

Ezra was a gazer who did exactly that. He was a man after God's heart who loved to study God's Word. Ezra and the Israelites were exiled after King Nebuchadnezzar ransacked Jerusalem. Many years later, after God softened the heart of King Artaxerxes, Jeremiah prophesied the return of the Israelites to their homeland. Ezra tells the story of the Israelites return to Jerusalem in Ezra 6-7.

I've just started reading Scripture. I feel closer to Jesus than ever before. —Kurt, 17

Ezra journeyed from Babylon to Jerusalem with thousands of other Jews. The Bible tells us Ezra was a teacher "well versed in the Law of Moses" (7:6). King Artaxerxes granted him return because "the hand of God was on him." But why was God's hand on him? Ezra "devoted himself to the study and observance to the

Law of Moses and to teaching its decrees and laws in Israel" (Ezra 7:10). I love that! Ezra was devoted to studying the law of God. And he didn't just read God's Word, he lived it. He taught it to others. Ezra is just one model of someone who lived and loved Scripture.

Heading out the Door with Scripture under Your Arm

In one of his letters to Timothy, Paul wrote, "All Scripture is God-breathed and useful for teaching, rebuking, correcting and training in righteousness, so all God's people may be thoroughly equipped for every good work" (2 Timothy 3:16). Did you catch what Paul says the purpose of Scripture is? Scripture's purpose is to *equip* you. It equips you for the real world you're entering. It equips you with God's wisdom. It helps you understand your story, your journey, is connected to the stories of so many others who've gone before you. It helps you look back so you can move forward in faith.

The author of the book of Hebrews says, "Remember your leaders, who spoke the word of God to you. Consider the outcome of their way of life and imitate their faith. Jesus Christ is the same yesterday, today and forever" (Hebrews 13:7-8). We have such a legacy to live; so many have gone before us.

So why do we have such a hard time reading and studying the connecting story our Creator has given us? Why don't we see Scripture as a *filet mignon* ready to be devoured? Why don't we savor it, mediate on it, *hagah* it, like my dog loves her bone?

> When I study Scripture, I feel like I can conquer anything. But sometimes it's hard to stay consistent in your walk with God.
> —Rachel, 15

I believe one reason is we don't really believe it gives us life. Even if we'd never say it out loud, we often think of the Bible as a dead book. We think it's just a collection of stories from the distant past. We don't really see it as alive.

But it is alive. It laughs with you, cries with you, and serves as a mirror and compass for your life. Your identity is revealed as you devour the stories of Scripture.

Some people eat and drink too fast. My five-year-old son loves to drink hot cocoa. Every time Levi is given a cup of cocoa he drinks it in one gulp. He doesn't even put the cup down. One gulp. Gone.

Many study Scripture this way: They go at it quickly. We need to slow down with Scripture, tasting, chewing, savoring, swallowing, and digesting it. We need to take these God-breathed words to heart, opening ourselves to change—and transformation. The Bible is your lifeline, your life-source. It's your identity in God. It's food for the soul.

Will you really get into reading and studying Scripture? Will you find your own story in God's story? It's your food. Your whole life after high school depends on it. Go *hagah*!

Questions for the Journey

1. On a scale of 1 to 10, with 10 being "I love it," how much do you enjoy reading the Bible?

2. How could you grow in your desire to study Scripture?

3. Do you see Scripture as just another book or a living, breathing companion? What difference do you think this makes in your motivation to read and study it?

4. What can you do this week to improve your Scripture study?

Web Resources

http://eword.gospelcom.net/year

Here's a great tool if you would like to read through the whole Bible. You can choose the version of the Bible and date you start and it sets you up with a reading plan.

bible.crosswalk.com

This Bible study resource site has tools for word study and other helps.

leestrobel.com

Author Lee Strobel's Web site is a great spot for articles and videos explaining the message of Jesus Christ and other theological issues with sound arguments.

Book Resources

Eat This Book: A Conversation in the Art of Spiritual Reading by Eugene H. Peterson (Eerdmans, 2006).

Understanding and Applying the Bible by Robertson McQuilkin (Moody, 1992).

The Life You've Always Wanted by John Ortberg (Zondervan, 2002).

My Utmost for His Highest by Oswald Chambers (Oswald Chambers Publications, 1993).

CHAPTER 2
BELIEF: YOUR IDENTITY IN JESUS

*Jesus is loving, caring, and awesome. He was the ultimate sacrifice.
Following Christ is like resting in our identity with him.
—Annabel, 15*

Custom Shading

Several summers ago, I was invited to speak at a youth-and-family camp in Pennsylvania. It was right in the middle of July, and it was brutally humid. In the mornings and early afternoons, we'd gather, and I'd encourage and challenge the students from Scripture. By the end of the afternoon session, not only were the students ready for a break, I was ready for some games in the great outdoors. When I speak at camps, I always try to get involved in the fun stuff too. I have no problem "suffering" for Jesus.

As you might imagine, we played a variety of games—including a few anything-goes, full-contact ones. They were unbelievably fun, but also a little dangerous. Do you know the kind of games I'm talking about?

One afternoon someone pulled out the water-balloon launcher. All the youth campers gathered in a pack on one end of the field as the counselors launched the balloons 40-some yards toward the group. Whoever caught the balloon shrapnel in the air got big points. Whoever got the most points was the winner. Easy, right?

It sounded fun, so I joined in the action. As the balloons came in, the most athletic, competitive, die-hard guys seemed to take over. Not wanting to be outdone, I jumped in with the rest of them and did my best to collect parts of balloon. Then...boom! I came down on top of one of the high school guys. To be precise, my top row of teeth came down on his head. Yes, it hurt, but I didn't make a big deal of it. (I told you I was suffering for Jesus.) I made sure he was okay, and the game continued.

The camp ended, and I returned home. On one of my first evenings back, my wife and I were sitting on the couch when she looked at me and said, "You have a crack on your front tooth." I didn't believe her, so I took a look for myself. Sure enough, my left front tooth was cracked. When I went to the dentist, he told me the bad news: "It's not a question of *whether* your tooth will fall out, but *when* your tooth will fall out." He said I needed a crown on my front tooth. (That's a fake tooth for all you who don't know dental terminology.) He said the crown would require a "custom shading."

Several days later, I found myself in the basement of a strange–smelling, laboratory-like house in some subdivision. This is where the custom shading would take place. A woman examined my teeth, took notes, and compared colors so the new tooth would match the old one.

I would describe Jesus as the perfect gift from heaven and role model to follow. Jesus is our Lord and Savior. He showed us how to live.
—Rachel, 15

Apparently, the shades of my teeth are so complicated that I needed the new tooth to be customized!

This reminded me of something. The color of my teeth isn't the only unique thing about me: I'm unique. I'm special. I'm unusual. I'm exceptional. And so are you. This isn't prideful thinking or talking. Our loving God uniquely created each one of us. What's more, when we surrender our lives to God and seek to follow Jesus, he does something exceptional in us: He makes us into something new. We're "born again," as Jesus explained to Nicodemus (John 3).

If you've given your life to Christ, the King of Kings has customized you: Your identity has changed. Like a caterpillar turned butterfly, you're beautifully made. You can fly in freedom. You're a new creation, not in the future, but now (1 Corinthians 5:17).

The Real You

Sometimes we trick ourselves into thinking we're not something special. Sometimes we beat ourselves up with guilt and grief. Especially during your teenage years, you might look in the mirror and dislike what you see. When we're not living faithful lives for God, the Holy Spirit will convict us and point us back to the right path with Jesus. But other times we need to be reminded who we are because of our relationship with Jesus, our position in Christ as a result of his grace. This free gift puts us in a special, customized place.

> Jesus is the ultimate example of love and a servant in action. Jesus loved us enough to spend 33 years on earth as a human without the comforts of being solely divine because he loves us.
> —Jimmy, 23

Years ago, I got the opportunity to walk the ruins of the biblical city of Ephesus in Turkey. We saw places where people worshipped false gods and a partially standing library with Greek inscriptions. I fantasized about taking one of those huge blocks of marble with cool Greek letters home with me, but it didn't happen.

The highlight of the trip was walking into the large theater where the city people would gather for dramas and city-council meetings. The book of Acts tells us that when Paul was in Ephesus, his truthful words about Jesus caused a riot. Paul had to quickly escape by boat to spare his life (Acts 19:21-31). Later Paul wrote a letter to the Ephesian Christians describing their real identity. That letter is what we now know as the book of Ephesians.

Paul's words to these believers can help us remember our true identity. It's almost as if there's a thread woven throughout the book that describes the real you in connection to Jesus. Let's look for it together.

> *Jesus is my rock and shield. —David, 18*

At the beginning of the letter, Paul stated he was writing to the saints of Ephesus (Ephesians 1:1). At first, this might seem strange. Maybe you've grown up in a tradition that uses the word *saints* to talk about holy people who've died. But Paul isn't writing to dead people; he's writing to people who are alive in Christ. Because of their relationship with Jesus, their real identity is that of a saint. That's true for you, too. God sees you as completely clean because Jesus died for your sins. *You are a saint.*

Paul points out that those who follow Jesus are blessed "with every spiritual blessing" (1:3). Do you feel blessed? He doesn't mean blessed with material possessions, but something greater. When you become a follower of Jesus, your insides change. Peace, comfort, and joy invade your heart. You move from darkness into light. These are spiritual blessings in Jesus. *You are blessed.*

Have you ever been chosen last? Maybe it was on the athletic field or in the classroom. Well, God reverses the order. The real you was chosen first. Paul tells us we were "chosen before the creation of the world" (1:4). No matter what your history, in God's heart you're chosen because you're extremely valuable. He loves you. *You are chosen first.*

One of my nieces is adopted. I still remember when my sister and brother-in-law went to pick up Abby. They had to make preparations, pay bills, and sign papers. Paul tells us we're "adopted by God" (1:5). For God, adoption is final. You and I cannot be unadopted. God will not turn his back on you. You are his child. *You are adopted.*

> *Following Jesus is doing what he has asked of us and doing as he would do. —Jodi, 15*

And as Paul reminds us a few verses later, God's forgiveness comes along with this adoption (1:7). Pastor and author John Piper says forgiveness is like a hug. Whenever my wife and I get into a disagreement—or what we sometime call "intense fellowship" (we don't argue)—I know we've reconciled when we finally hug. It's only when she and I face each other and embrace that I know full forgiveness has taken effect. The moment we ask God to take away our sins through Jesus' death on the cross, we're free. *You are forgiven.*

Alive in the Spirit

Has anyone ever asked you to do something without giving you the stuff necessary to do it? Maybe your friend asked you to wash his car, but didn't give you a hose, soap, sponge, and towel to accomplish the job (or quarters to use in the automatic car wash). Well, Paul assures us God doesn't do that. He tells the Ephesians—and us—we've been given all we need to follow Jesus. Paul tells us we're "marked in him with a seal, the promised Holy Spirit" (1:13). God doesn't ask you to live without a counselor, leader, and friend to guide you along the path of life. *You have been tattooed with the Holy Spirit.*

And in that Spirit, Paul tells us we've been made "alive in Christ" (2:5). I don't understand why some who follow after Jesus seem to be dead on their feet. One of the reasons Jesus died was for us to be alive. The real you isn't comatose but overflowing with the fruit of the spirit (Galatians 5). *You are alive.*

I'm sure the Ephesian followers of Jesus must have been depressed sometimes. Like each of us, they must've occasionally felt down in the dumps and forgotten their identity. But Paul reminds them, and all who follow Jesus, that we've "been raised up with Christ" (2:6). The moment we chose to follow Jesus, we were lifted to a new playing field. We were in the street, but now we're in the stronghold. Our heads were down, but now they're up. No matter what your outward circumstances, you've been raised from death to life just as Jesus was raised from the dead (Philippians 3). *You've been lifted up.*

Paul also tells the Ephesian followers of Christ they've been given a special gift: grace. He says, "You have received God's saving grace" (2:8). Think about the gifts you receive on Christmas morning. When was the last time you received a gift you earned and deserved? I love Christmas because it's a time when grace is expressed—most of the gifts given on this great holiday are given for free with nothing asked for in return. In the same manner, salvation is yours because of Jesus' grace. It was unearned and undeserved. You had nothing to do with it. *You are full of grace.*

> Jesus is God and Jesus is God's son. Jesus is loving and full of grace. Those who follow Jesus are attempting to follow the example he gave us while he was here and are living to worship him.
> —Deb, 28

God's Handiwork

In the last chapter, I told you a bit about my visit to the Louvre with some students. For hours, many of us took in the sculptures and pieces of antiquity, including a number of Grecian works from Paul's time. Perhaps we looked at some of the same artwork Paul had in mind when he wrote the church in Ephesus, saying, "You are God's workmanship" (2:10).

Look in the mirror and tell yourself, "I was made by the hands of God." It really is amazing to think that the God of the entire universe took the time to knit each one of us together before we were ever born. He cared enough to number the hairs on your head, color your hair, design your nose, place your ears, dye your eyes, paint your face, and position your lips—and that's just your head. *You are a work of art.*

But you're not just a body—you're also a spiritual being who has "direct access" to God (2:18). How amazing is that? It's like God has given us a backstage pass. As a result of our relationship with Jesus, we now have something hanging around our hearts that gives us permission to go to God anytime we'd like. It's called the Spirit. Because we have the Holy Spirit living inside of us, the real you can communicate with the Creator of the universe. In fact, Paul goes on to say that we may "approach God with freedom and confidence" (3:12). That's something special. *You have access to God through prayer.*

Your Place in the World

I'm grateful to be a citizen of the United States. This residency is special, but it's nothing compared to Paul's words to the Christians in Ephesus about their place in the world. He says, "You are no longer foreigners or strangers, but fellow citizens with God's people and members of his household" (2:19). You might sometimes feel like you're out of place in this world, but Paul says we're connected to a family of believers in Jesus called the Church. *You are connected to community.*

Finally, toward the end of Paul's letter to the Ephesians, he shares with them, "You are righteous and holy" (4:24). The apostle comes full circle, ending the letter where he began it. The divine thread of the "real you" started back in the very first verse of the book with a single word: *Saint*. And in verse 4:24, he defines that word: "like God in true righteousness and holiness." Being right before God by grace through faith in Jesus puts us in a place of holiness. In God's eyes, you're holy. Can you believe that? We are set apart for Jesus. As a result, you can be confident in your position in Jesus. *You are set apart.*

Your real identity is in Jesus. This makes you out-of-the-ordinary. In another one of his letters, Paul reminds believers that the mystery of Jesus Christ was made known to them. Not only that but the God of the universe, who came to earth in human form, lives inside of them—and inside of you (Colossians 1:27). This should give you great hope and excitement as you follow Jesus for the long haul. *This is the real you.*

Questions for the Journey

1. Think about a time when you were one of the last ones chosen for a team or task. How did it make you feel? How does it feel to know you've been chosen first by God?

2. What makes it so difficult for us to realize how special we are in God's sight? Why do you think it's so hard for us to be content with who God designed us to be?

3. Look back at the italicized phrases at the end of each paragraph. Which of the descriptions of the real you is most challenging for you to accept? What could you do this week to "nail down" your identity in Jesus?

Web Resources

Web Presentations about Jesus Christ:

> *believeinjesus.com/index.htm*

> *matthiasmedia.com.au/2wtl/*

> *crosswalk.com/whoIsJesus/1346092/*

> *whoisjesus-really.com/main.htm*

> *navpress.com/dj.asp*
>> *Discipleship Journal* helps Christians of all ages understand the Scriptures and apply them to life.

> *christianityworks.com*
>> This site is offered by a division of the Back to the Bible organization. The site calls itself "the ultimate interactive quest online" and has the goal of bringing young people to knowledge and acceptance of Jesus Christ.

Book Resources

Great Lives: Jesus: The Greatest Life of All by Charles R. Swindoll (Thomas Nelson, 2008).

The Jesus Creed: Loving God, Loving Others by Scot McKnight (Paraclete Press, 2007).

The Case for Christ (Student Edition) by Jane Vogel and Lee Strobel (Zondervan, 2001).

Excavating Jesus by John Dominic Crossan (HarperCollins, 2002).

CHAPTER 3
DOUBT: YOUR IDENTITY IN UNCERTAINTY

Everyone doubts. No matter how strong your faith, sometimes you get that feeling that God just isn't real. If you don't struggle with that, then I doubt you're really chasing him. It's doubt that makes faith stronger, when you're lying in your bed wondering why you're praying—and you keep praying anyway because your faith is more than feelings. —David, 18

A Disciple's Hesitation

It happened. It was done. Finished. Complete. Fulfilled. The proof had been on display with eyewitness accounts for more than 40 days (Acts 1:3). *Forty days!* That's longer than a month. That's longer than Christmas break.

Jesus' closest friends had seen him repeatedly after the resurrection. They knew he'd been crucified, yet there he was again—alive. Put yourself in their sandals for a minute or two. Can you imagine seeing him again? You might have hugged him, shared a meal with him, laughed with him, cried with him, and heard him retell stories of events you'd seen firsthand. "Remember that storm on the lake?" he would say. "Remember the faith of Peter?"

As he spoke, you couldn't stop starring at him. As he served you the bread on the beach (John 21:13), you couldn't help staring at the holes in his hands. He was walking among you again. There was no reason for you to doubt the tomb was empty and Jesus was alive.

But according to Matthew, some of those closest to Jesus *did* doubt. Listen to his account of one of the final commissioning speeches from Jesus to his disciples:

> Then the eleven disciples went to Galilee, to the mountain where Jesus had told them to go. When they saw him, they worshipped him; but some doubted. (Matthew 28:16-17)

Remember, this isn't the first time the disciples spent time with Jesus after he rose from the dead; they'd been with him before. One time it was with a crowd of 500 (1 Corinthians 15:6)! Yet Matthew tells us some doubted. *Some doubted?* Why? How? These men and women had been with Jesus off and on for over forty days. Yet they still had this place deep inside that questioned, that wondered, "Could all this be true? Is Jesus really alive in front of me? Is Jesus really the Messiah?"

I never have doubts about following him. My doubts usually lie to me and tell me I'm not doing this Christian walk right. I feel insecure, inadequate, as if I'm not equipped to serve the Lord or I'm not smart enough. But usually when I get back to God I'm more secure and reassured; I'm just where he wants me.
—Annie, 29

And what about Thomas? He's mainly known as a doubter—a bummer of a description to have written on his tombstone. But his first reaction to hearing the news that the other disciples had seen Jesus alive was, "No way! I've got to see it myself." Nothing happened for a week. *A week!* Thomas might've laid awake thinking about it every night of the week, his doubts growing deeper each dark minute.

Then, a week later, Jesus appears to the disciples again—and this time Thomas was there (John 20:24-29). Jesus set up a personal worship experience with him. I can imagine Jesus telling Thomas something like, "Tom, come over here and put your fingers in the holes in my hands. Put your fingers in my side. Feel that? That's from the spikes and spear. What do you think, Tom?" John tells us that doubting Thomas responded, "My Lord and my God!"

Do you think Thomas ever doubted again? We don't really know. Maybe he did. But on that day he understood the true identity of Jesus.

> *I have doubts about God when "good people" do stupid things which have bad consequences and it kind of seems like God doesn't care. Then I read similar problems in the Bible and, in the end, God always had a good solution.*
> *—Jodi, 15*

What to Do with Doubts

Doubts about spiritual things come in all shapes and sizes. There are big doubts that plague all of us and hang around for a while. There are smaller doubts that quickly come and go. I can imagine sometimes when you've prayed you've felt like the prayers just bounced off the ceiling. I know I've had that feeling. You might be questioning if you're heading to the right college or landing the right job. Maybe you're wondering why that terrible tragedy happened or questioning whether God even cares about the details of your life.

Doubts make their way in. You can do your best to ignore them and get past them, but they keep knocking at the door of your heart. As a believer in Jesus, you might think, *I'm not supposed to doubt, right?* You might feel like others look to you for answers, but you're filled with questions of your own. You begin to beat yourself up with guilt. *What's wrong with me? Why do I doubt God? I'm a believer. What will my friends and family think of me?*

If you're struggling with doubt, I'd encourage you to relax. Take a deep breath. Doubts are a normal part of the journey with Jesus, and they're especially common in times of transition. As you journey out the door, customizing your life into all that God would have it become, you'll face doubts. But your identity is in Christ, and placing your faith in him will help you work through those doubts.

> *In the back of my mind, it often still seems too good to be true. Or I doubt my adequacy or worthiness to be one of his sheep. Why did he choose me? In the past year I've learned Jesus will accept me for who I am. Why can't I do that? He accepts all of me. God is love. This is a very simple, but profound revelation.*
> *—Rob, 26*

Remember: Doubt is not the opposite of belief. The opposite of belief is *unbelief*. Authentic faith says, "I doubt like the rest, and I'll be honest with my feelings." I think the disciples were honest about their doubts, and Jesus helped them along as they kept following him. Maybe he had to hang around for 40 days after the resurrection just so they'd be convinced he was alive! The key is to stay true to your deep belief in God and follow Jesus wholeheartedly, even when doubts creep in. Don't run away from God when you doubt; use it as an opportunity to get closer to Jesus like Thomas did. Get close enough to touch his hands and side.

Deal with Doubt

Here are some tips to help you handle those times when you find yourself struggling with doubt.

First, acknowledge the doubt. Don't deny it. Don't be embarrassed. It's normal to doubt. Think about the most mature

Jesus-followers you know—the people you most admire and look to because of how they love Jesus and people. There's a good chance those folks have experienced doubt at times. Share your questions with them and ask them to share how they've dealt with their own doubts. I hope they can admit some of their doubts to you. If they can't, then they're not being real with you. It's worse to pretend you don't doubt. Give yourself room to think through your questions and struggles.

> *Most of my doubting comes in at the most likely place: Could Jesus really be the Son of God? It's hard to for anyone to comprehend God himself coming to Earth in human form. I deal with this through prayer, asking God to remove my doubtful thoughts. —Jaclyn, 17*

Second, admit your doubts to God. Don't just lie awake at night worrying. Talk to him. Tell him your feelings. He's God. Just like any other relationship, your relationship with God will grow with communication. Tell him your doubts in your own words. You won't shock him—he already knows your thoughts and the feelings of your heart. So just go ahead and claim them. Ask him to walk with you through the dark valley of doubt.

Third, go to good resources. Take some time in the Scripture with your questions. In the back of most study Bibles is a concordance that includes some key themes and Scripture verses on various topics. Do your questions line up with some of these topics? Look them up in the Scriptures. Many people of the Bible have already asked the same questions of doubt.

Fourth, nail down the essentials of your belief in Jesus—the real certainties. You and I don't know everything there is to know about God—we know about a thimble's worth of the universe's understanding of God. You may never receive answers to all your questions and doubts this side of heaven, and that's where faith in God comes into play. Authentic followers of Jesus live with the tension and mystery that God is God and we're not. Continue striving to know God, but recognize there are some things you might not know this side of eternity. When you doubt, make a list of the essentials of your faith in Jesus. Hold on to this list for a rainy day. When doubts and doubters come along, remind yourself of the most important things.

Doubts will come and go. Admit you have them. Talk to God, talk to good friends, and understand the most important aspects of your faith in Jesus. Dwell on him. Fill your mind with true, noble, right, pure, lovely, admirable, excellent, and praiseworthy things (Philippians 4:8).

Remember, God really is in control—even when you don't understand what he's doing. That's why I'm so glad he's God and I'm not, otherwise I would've messed it all up a long time ago. God is the God of answers, but sometimes I think he thought up all the questions, too—so ask away. There's no question he hasn't already dwelled on. He would love to journey with you and your doubts.

Questions for the Journey

1. Do you see doubting as good or bad? Do you think it's okay to doubt some things as a follower of Jesus?

2. Can you identify areas that are causing doubt in your life?

3. What are some ways you can bring peace to your doubts this week? How can God help you?

Web Resources

relevantmagazine.com

A voice for the next generation with articles on God, life, and culture.

christianitytoday.com/teens/features/selfesteem.html
> *Christianity Today* has a great link for teenagers called "Ignite your Faith."

Book Resources

Mirror, Mirror: Reflections on Who You Are and Who You'll Become by Kara Powell and Kendall Payne (Zondervan, 2003).

Living with Questions by Dale Fincher (Zondervan, 2007).

Faith and Doubts by John Ortberg (Zondervan, 2008).

Be Last by Jeremy Kingsley (Tyndale, 2008).

CHAPTER 4
DESIGN: YOUR IDENTITY IN GOD'S WILL

We all need to stay connected to God and use the gifts he's given us. —Ryan, 24

It All Starts in Kindergarten

One day I went to visit my daughter's kindergarten classroom. It's such a joy to spend time watching a group of five-year-olds closely.

At one desk there was a little girl absorbed in finger painting. Her eyes were bright with excitement over the mix of colors and the feel of the paints on her hands.

Over in the corner two boys were building a tower with blocks. One of them stacked the blocks rapidly with little care for the finished product. The other boy went out of his way to straighten up the messy construction made by the first. They needed no supervision.

Out on the playground was the class prankster. He loved to take the ball from the girls. He'd run around in victory like he'd captured a great treasure. He hoped to provoke a response, but his audience seemed more annoyed than anything.

Back in the classroom was a child sitting all by herself, looking at a book. It's not that she was shy, sad, or bored. She loved time by herself and was content all alone.

Fast-forward with me into the future. Let's imagine we could meet up with all these kids a few years after they've graduated from college. Let's assume they're all Christians, seriously committed to following Jesus. They're customizing their lives according to God's will.

Remember the little finger-painting girl? As an adult, she works as a buyer of textiles for a clothing manufacturer. She loves to arrange colors and patterns.

The two boys who were building with blocks are headed into the corporate world. One is a salesman bent on exceeding performance goals. The other will always be a refiner—a straightening-things-up, maximizing-effectiveness sort of guy. He works as a project manager at a nonprofit organization.

The class prankster? He's a youth pastor. His love of joking around and turning heads (and his desire to be the center of attention) is now used to reach people.

Finally, there's the girl in the corner who loved solitude and silence. She's now a magazine editor who has just written her first book.

All of these kids took the skills and interests they had as children, honed and refined them over time, and today use those gifts for God's glory. They've all discovered the will of God for their lives: The way he designed each one, the way he wants each one to be.[2]

God's Will for You

What do you remember loving to do as a child? Did you like to play with friends? Go fishing? Write poems? Tell jokes? Build things? Use your imagination? Draw pictures? Win games? Make new friends? Read? Help mom and dad landscape the yard? Talk to squirrels?

The point of all this questioning is this: God placed certain interests inside of you. It was his idea. It wasn't a mistake. The psalmist declares to God:

> I praise you because I am fearfully and wonderfully made; your works are wonderful, I know that full well. My frame was not hidden from you when I was made in the secret place. When I was woven together in the depths of the earth, your eyes saw my unformed body. All the days ordained for me were written in your book before one of them came to be. (Psalm 139:14-16)

The desires in the hearts of those kindergarteners are no accident. God formed each and every one of those children in his or her mother's womb. It's the same with you. He formed you and knows you. He has a specific plan for you, and he's been preparing you to fulfill this plan. You were created by God's hands for God's glory. After coming to know Jesus as the Lord of your life, he now has good works planned for you to do on his divine calendar. The awesome thing is those good works are often in line with your heart's desires—maybe

God will show you his plan for your life. Keep your eyes open.
—Rachel, 15

2 This illustration was inspired by my own experiences with my children and the stories in Arthur F. Miller Jr.'s book *Why You Can't Be Anything You Want To Be* (Zondervan, 1999).

even the same desires you had back in kindergarten. That's how God designed you.

A Savory Buffet

You've probably wondered: *What am I going to do with the rest of my life? What's God's purpose for me?* These questions about God's will for your life are very important. But I think we sometimes feel paralyzed by them. We're afraid of missing out on God's plan for us. We're rolling along on the highway of life, and we're afraid the path to God's will for us is a single, tiny dirt road marked by a single, weather-beaten sign. We're afraid we might miss our exit and never find our way to the purpose God has in mind for us!

It's very important to keep our eyes and hearts open for the signs that can point us toward God's hopes and dreams for us. We'll talk more about that later.

But I don't believe God's will for each one of us is only found along a single path that's easy to miss. I think God's will for us is more like a buffet at the nicest restaurant in town. Can you picture it? It's like a huge table stretching as far you can see, with every possible appetizer, main course, and dessert available. It doesn't get any better than this! It's all God's will and he's saying, "Come eat. Start where you would like and eat till your heart's content." Is this the way you picture the will of God for your life? Or do you see it more like a cheap, fast-food meal with little freedom to choose (two options: with ketchup or without)?

I used to think God's will for me was very specific. I was supposed to be a teacher at a Christian school (I'm not), coach soccer (I don't), live in Michigan

> God reveals his will when you spend time with him in prayer and in his word. God will also speak to you through those around you, which makes it very important to find a community of believers and mentors that can speak truth into your life.
> —John, 23

(no again), get married (I did!), have two children (add one more), adopt a dog (check), and live in a house with a white-picket fence (a house, yes, but no fence). I thought if I were anything else, I would be out of the will of God. Do you know what I mean? Maybe you've felt the same way—living in fear of missing God's will instead of feeling the freedom to live in it. I've since changed my mind. The more I get to know the heart of the Father by studying the Scripture and daily experiencing his goodness, the more I'm convinced his will is a buffet. God is saying, "Eat till your stomach is satisfied, and then enjoy some more of me." I hope I'm creating freedom in your heart. God knows the plans he has for you. For God that plan may be very specific, but for us it should seem like a buffet of options (Ephesians 2:10). We're simply to live in obedience to all he asks us to do based on the Scripture and the Holy Spirit's direction. God has prepared a wonderful meal for you. So go get your buffet on!

Do you still have questions? Maybe I'm not being specific enough. You might wonder where to start eating off the buffet. Do you start with the appetizer, main course, or desert? Maybe you're afraid you're eating out of the dumpster behind the restaurant without realizing it. Let me give you some guidelines to calm your fears and give you confidence. Let's walk together through several scriptural principles that address God's will for your life. Pray and meditate on them as you read.

> *Just stay open to the things he shows you. Eventually, it'll all come together and then you'll know what you have to do. —Shae, 18*

Direction

It all starts with our desire to do the will of God. Some of those heading into the adult world don't have a heart's desire to live for God. The psalmist declared, "I desire to do your will, O my God; your law is within my heart" (Psalm 40:8). We need to humbly open ourselves up to learning like the psalmist did when he wrote, "Teach me to do your will, for you are my God; may your good

Spirit lead me on level ground" (Psalm 143:10). We need to ask God to help us know where his buffet is located and where the boundaries between good food and spoiled food lie. This is a heart check for us: Do we really desire to do God's will, to eat from the buffet by following Jesus for the long haul?

With this desire to eat from God's buffet and an understanding that God will guide us to where the "good food" is located, we can now live in his will. Living in the center of God's will is about becoming holy, or "set apart" (1 Thessalonians 4:3-8). This means becoming more like Jesus and actively seeking to set yourself apart for God in your choices and relationships.

God wants us to identify with Jesus in every area of our lives. This will certainly involve bringing others to the buffet and serving them along the way. When we see a need, we're to jump in and serve. This is what loving God and loving others is all about (Mark 10:43, John 13). This is being in the center of God's will.

Getting Specific

Following Jesus for the long haul means taking God's words to heart. It means needing God like our bodies need air and water. The writer of Proverbs echoes this sentiment:

> My son, if you accept my words and store up my commands within you, turning your ear to wisdom and applying your heart to understanding, and if you call out for insight and cry aloud for understanding, and if you look for it as for silver and search for it as for hidden treasure, then you will understand the fear of the Lord and find the knowledge of God. (Proverbs 2:1-5)

Another Proverb that gives us insight into God's desire for us reads, "Trust in the Lord with all your heart and lean not on your own understanding. In all your ways acknowledge him, and he will make your paths straight" (Proverbs 3:5-6). In other words, live your life for Jesus by obeying his teachings and living a life of service to him. Do this and he'll give you clear direction for your journey.

Sticking close to Jesus isn't always easy as you head into the unknown after high school. Difficulty is ahead of you. There may be times when you feel alone, but that's when you most need to lean on God's promises tucked away in Scripture.

In Romans Paul writes that we're to offer ourselves as "living sacrifices." Even when it gets hot and uncomfortable, we need to die to ourselves and live for God. If we do this, we're worshipping. And in doing this, Paul promises that we'll know God's will for our lives.

> Therefore, I urge you, brothers, in view of God's mercy, to offer your bodies as living sacrifices, holy and pleasing to God—this is your spiritual act of worship. Do not conform any longer to the pattern of this world, but be transformed by the renewing of your mind. Then you will be able to test and approve what God's will is—his good, pleasing and perfect will. (Romans 12:1-2)

God's Specific Will for You

Do you want to know God's will for your life? Stop and think about that question. Do you want to find your God-given sweet spot?

If the answer is yes, you're already eating from the buffet. As you grow closer to God and serve people for the long haul, God will reveal gifts, passions, talents, and dreams to you. As part of the body of Christ, God will give you opportunities to use the gifts you've been given for his purposes. Listen to Paul continue in that same chapter of Romans:

For by the grace given me I say to every one of you:
Do not think of yourself more highly than you ought,
but rather think of yourself with sober judgment, in
accordance with the faith God has distributed to each
of you. For just as each of us has one body with many
members, and these members do not all have the same
function, so in Christ we, though many, form one body,
and each member belongs to all the others. We have
different gifts, according to the grace given to each of us.
If your gift is prophesying, then prophesy in accordance
with your faith; if it is serving, then serve; if it is teaching,
then teach; if it is to encourage, then give encouragement;
if it is giving, then give generously; if it is to lead, do it
diligently; if it is to show mercy, do it cheerfully. (Romans
12:3-8)

Paul is telling you to stay humble and evaluate the gifts
and abilities God has given you. This process takes time as you
serve and try new areas of ministry. Ministry isn't just a job for full-
time pastors and missionaries; God wants every follower of Jesus to
discover and use his or her gifts.

The moment you surrendered
your life to Jesus, you were given gifts
to use to advance the kingdom. We all
need to discover these gifts as we serve
in the local church, campus ministry, and
everyday life. These gifts are connected
to passions, desires, dreams, natural
abilities, and talents.

I pray and listen to God, looking for signs that lineup with the situation. —Brooke, 17

God's specific will for your life is already planned. Just relax
and live for him. Continue to discover what it means to eat off
the center of the buffet by talking to him continually, reading the
Scriptures consistently, and obeying always. How fulfilling is that?
Doesn't this take a load off your shoulders? It's only after looking
back on a portion of our lives that we see clearly how God was
guiding us in his divine direction.

Rest in the fact that God has a specific future in mind for you that incorporates your passions, dreams, gifts, and natural talents for maximum Kingdom impact. Surrender, serve, and pursue God with all you've got. God promises to do the rest.

Questions for the Journey

1. Growing up, what did you know about the will of God?

2. Did any of the verses we've looked at in this chapter stick out to you, challenge you, or help you? Which ones? Why?

3. How are you seeking God's general will for your life?

4. How are you seeking God's specific will for your life?

5. Try making a list of your passions, dreams, gifts, and talents. How do they point to your God-given design?

Web Resources

http://christiancollegeguide.net

This is one of many college information finder sites. It includes all the latest information on Christian colleges—everything from cost to the spiritual life of the campus.

renovare.org

This is Richard Foster's site with articles and strategies to help your relationship with Jesus grow.

christianitytoday.com

Here's a good site featuring articles on following Jesus for the long haul. It also includes "Out of Ur," a resource designed for teenagers and young adults.

Book Resources

Why You Can't Be Anything You Want To Be by Arthur Miller (Zondervan, 1999).

The Divine Conspiracy by Dallas Willard (HarperCollins, 1998).

The Grand Weaver by Ravi Zacharias (Zondervan, 2008).

A Long Obedience in the Same Direction by Eugene Peterson (InterVarsity, 2000).

Knowing God by J.I. Packer (InterVarsity, 1993).

PART TWO:

CHOICES - Do My Decisions Matter?

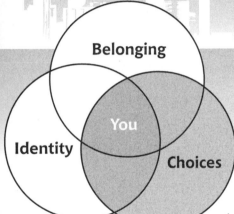

I do my best to follow Jesus and try hard to make the right choices all the time. —Bradley, 16

As you move on from high school, you'll gain a greater amount of power and control over your life. You'll have more freedom to make your own decisions. You probably long for such freedom, but there's a cost that comes with it. With this new freedom comes increased responsibility for your decisions and actions. And like so many great action movies illustrate, power can be used for good or bad, for productivity or destruction.

You're in the middle of a shift in power, control, and responsibility. You'll increasingly make the big decisions in your life and probably have mixed feelings about this. On one hand, you probably can't wait to be on your own and away from the boundaries of the people who raised you. On the other hand, the people and structures you've been depending on until this point will no longer be present in the same way. This might make you nervous, at least a little. Take a look at what a couple of people said as they looked back on that time of transition to life after high school:

> *I'm in the first months of my transition to college, and it's much less dramatic than I expected. The hardest part is establishing myself as a follower of Jesus all over again to these new people. I had a large amount of freedom in high school, at least my junior and senior years, because I'd earned my parents' trust. This made the transition a lot easier. —David, 18*

> *No matter how well you do in high school, or how great your friends are, it's not easy going to college and suddenly having all of this freedom (which is terrific) and responsibility (which can be good, too). In high school, it was easy for me to shine because I had this amazing support network of friends and adults. You really have to build a new network of support after high school when you're suddenly separated from your childhood friends and family. —Deb, 28*

In this section, we'll talk about what good choices look like. I'll set you up to cruise into the real world and not crash and burn into adulthood. It's up to you to make the right choices, take on more responsibility, and wisely handle the new power you have.

CHAPTER 5

RESPONSIBILITY: YOUR CHOICES OF WISDOM

Surrounding myself with positive people who love Christ makes it easier to live my life better. I hate disappointing my parents, friends, and family, so thinking about things and their consequences helps me make the right choices. I pray that God will help me make those right choices in my whole life and that he'll be with me each step I take. —Candice, 17

So Many Choices

Every human being has something in common: We all have the power of choice. We all get to determine the direction of our own lives.

My chocolate lab, Mocha, doesn't have that same capacity to choose. Yes, she can decide when she wants to eat or sleep, but she never carries the same level of responsibility we do. She just lies around all day, mostly on our couch. Once in a while she'll open an eye, eat some dog food, or take a walk, but she mostly sleeps. There are moments when I think being Mocha would be great. But in the end I think having the free will to make choices is one of the greatest gifts God gives us.

As you leave high school, the world is your oyster. This is such an exciting time for you! The options are endless. The will of God is laid out in front of you like a Sunday buffet ready to be devoured. So why is there so much stress?

The stress likely comes from a number of sources, but it mostly stems from the importance and sheer number of choices to be made. With choices comes the "r" word. You know it. Go ahead and say it out loud. *Responsibility.* Some choices will happen quickly, some have already happened, and others won't come until you get down the road a bit. But the big choices you're making, and the responsibility that goes with them, are multiplying.

Everything boils down to choices. Some people choose to smoke, drink, party, ski, chat online, snowboard, email, vacation, talk on the cell phone, do drugs, or have sex now and think about the consequences later. These are all choices, some bigger than others. In the end your life is the sum total of your choices made.

God created you to live a full and healthy life. He wants to help you make wise choices. Paul wrote to the church in Ephesus, "Be very careful, then, how you live—not as unwise but as wise, making the most of every opportunity, because the days are evil" (Ephesians 5:15-16). God wants to give us more and more wisdom so we can live the full life that Jesus came to give each and every one (John 10:10).

I try my best not to be selfish and not ask others, "What can you do for me?" but "What can I do for you?"—Ryan, 24

Little Leads to Big

Wise little decisions lead to wise big decisions. Read that again. As you make the leap from high school to college and beyond, you'll face all kinds of choices daily. If you're going to college, you'll decide how your dorm room is arranged, how you schedule your days, when you study, when you sleep, what habits you'll establish, whom you go out with on the weekends, how often you call home, how many meals to eat a day, how often to do laundry...you get the point.

Some of these choices might not seem like a big deal, but let's think about laundry for a minute. If you decide to wait to do laundry until all your socks are stinky, you may be forced to wear flip-flops to class. You might think, *What's wrong with that? I love flip-flops!* Well, there's nothing wrong with them as long as you're not in the middle of a winter snowstorm. But unless you have fur on your toes, you'll probably want socks when you're walking in snow. I think you get the point. If you make a dumb little decision, like waiting till the last possible second to do your laundry, you may pay later.

If you make wise decisions about the little things in your life, you'll have a much easier time making the wise decisions when the big things come along. Laundry might be a small choice, but paying off your credit card every month, deciding to get married, or buying a home or a car are bigger choices you'll need to take responsibility for later. Develop the habit of being faithful in the little things. This will grow your wisdom for the bigger decisions later.

> *It's important to have good friends who keep me accountable for my choices. —Jodi, 15*

Making Smart Choices

As you grow in responsibility, here are some tips about making wise choices as you follow Jesus.

First, remember God is the source of true wisdom, and the Bible is his big story—his grand narrative. Start reading the stories of Scripture asking, "What does this teach me about God and his wisdom? How can I apply this wisdom to my everyday life?" The book of Proverbs is full of wisdom to help you make the right choices. Try reading a chapter a day for the next month—there are 31 chapters in all.

Second, before you make a big decision, seek the advice of a few Jesus-following adult friends or mentors. (See the chapter on *Mentoring*). Be honest and open with them. Share your thoughts and feelings about the choice to be made. Allow them to pray with you and for you over a period of time before making the choice. Listen to their advice and take it to heart.

Third, take a look in the mirror. As you grow into a mature, Jesus-following adult, manage your time wisely, and take responsibility for your life, you'll need to be honest with yourself. Growing in maturity entails taking a careful look at the real you and the choices you're making. You might be able to trick yourself easier than you can trick others. Be authentic. Be real. As you consider any decision, honestly ask yourself: *Will the choice I'm about to make help me love Jesus and love others better?*

Fourth, take a look at God. We all need to pray about the choices we face. God knows you best and has your best interest in mind. He loves you, and you need to hide this deep in your identity. God is the King who has authority over your life, but he's also a dad who's tender and compassionate toward his children. He's the King Daddy. You may need to pray about some choices for a few days or a few weeks; some choices may even require months or years of prayer. This might seem like forever, but the older you get, the faster time flies. An hour seems like a few minutes.

> *I try to love God and love others. It's really hard sometimes.*
> *—Billy, 16*

Fifth, stay patient. Listen for God's voice as you pray. Only a few people have heard God's audible voice; you might hear his voice as a still, small impression of peace in your heart. Jesus says his sheep know his voice because they've spent time with the Good Shepherd (John 10:1-18). Turn up your spiritual hearing aid. Pull out those spiritual Q-tips. Await God's response.

> *I set goals for myself and then reach those goals. —Jodi, 15*

The Ultimate Example of Responsibility

Jesus spent his time doing things that really mattered. He lived his life moment-by-moment as a model for us. Needless to say, Jesus was responsible and made wise decisions. He touched people. He healed people. He talked to people others shunned. He laughed with outcasts. He cried with sinners. He made time for people (Luke 10:30-37). He loved to hang out with his friends and celebrate, too. After long days with the crowds and his disciples, Jesus would often get up early to pray for the day ahead (Mark 1:35). Did you know Jesus led a seminar on time management? Okay, maybe not a real 21st-century seminar, but he used teachable moments to show his disciples how to best use their time.

Do you remember the story of Mary and Martha? Jesus and the disciples came to the sisters' home. Upon walking through the door, Jesus noticed Martha frantically running around from task to task, like a chicken with its head cut off. Mary chose to spend her time at the feet of Jesus, listening to stories and fellowshipping with the disciples. When Martha started to complain that Mary wasn't working, Jesus told her, "Martha, Martha, you are worried and upset about many things, but few things are needed—or indeed only one. Mary has chosen what is better, and it will not be taken away from her" (Luke 10:38-42).

According to Jesus, Mary got it right. Time is better spent with Jesus than focusing on temporal things. That's not license for you to tell your friend, "No, I can't help you clean the church because I'm reading my Bible." But it does mean you need to take Jesus with you *all day* so you can live every moment for him. Paul declares,

"Make the most of every opportunity. Let your conversation be always full of grace, seasoned with salt..." (Colossians 4:5-6).

The Wisest Choice

Many people ask the wrong question when it comes to making the smart choices. They ask, "Is anything wrong with this choice?" The better question is, "Is this the wisest thing for me to do?" If we want to be mature followers of Jesus, we need to take our focus off what's wrong and put our focus on God. To consistently make wise choices, you'll need to have a growing relationship with God.

I surround myself with people who'll keep me focused and not attempt to lead me astray. —Shae, 18

The way to discern the wisest thing to do is to spend time with the Wisest One. Make a commitment, now, to spend time with him everyday for the long haul.

I've heard it said that the person who kills time injures eternity. In other words, time wasted with poor choices has a negative impact on God's kingdom. As you grow into a spiritually mature adult, use your time wisely.

Take time to stop and think; it's a source of power.

Take time to play; it's the secret to staying young.

Take time to read the Word; it's the fountain of wisdom.

Take time to pray; it has the potential to change your life with God.

Take time to love and be loved; it's the way God designed you.

Take time to be friendly to everyone; it's the road to happiness.

Take time to laugh out loud; it's music to your soul.

Take time to give of yourself; life is too short to be selfish.

Take time to work hard; it's your response to all God has given you.

Take time and responsibility seriously as you leave high school and begin following Jesus for the long haul.

Questions for the Journey

1. How do you discern what choices are wise?

2. Where does wisdom come from? How does God's perspective on wisdom differ from the world's?

3. Is it easier for you to ask "Is there anything wrong with this?" or "Is this a wise thing for me to do?" What's the difference?

4. How important are friends in helping you make smart decisions?

Web Resources

dwillard.org

Dallas Willard's site features articles and strategies for growing in your relationship with Jesus.

wired.com

The daily technology updates on this Web site can help you to consider the future, daring you to think for the rest of your life.

planetwisdom.com

Author Mark Matlock has a good resource for growing in responsibility and wisdom as you make the transition from high school to college and beyond.

Book Resources

Wisdom On...Making Good Decisions by Mark Matlock (Zondervan, 2008).

What's So Amazing About Grace? by Philip Yancey (Zondervan, 2008).

Smart Girls Think Twice: Making Wise Choices When It Counts by Jan Silvious (Thomas Nelson, 2008).

Freshman by Mark Matlock (NavPress, 2005).

CHAPTER 6
MORALITY: YOUR CHOICES OF BEHAVIOR

The Bible is full of references to morality and immorality, purity and impurity. No, it might not address every specific issue on morality, but you can definitely get God's overall view of what his standard looks like from reading his Word. —Adam, 23

Mind your P's and Q's

What is morality, anyway? The dictionary defines *morality* as "a set of standards of conduct that are accepted as right or proper." But what about Christian morality? Is that any different? Should those who follow Jesus have different standards of morality than those who do not know Jesus as their Lord?

Each culture and society has its own set of written and unwritten rules, its own opinions as to what's right or authoritative. For example, most modern cultures would agree that murder is unacceptable behavior. But people might disagree about whether or not it's okay to steal from a grocery store if you need food, take revenge on a mean neighbor, or drink alcohol. Even within the body of Christ, we don't all agree on all issues of morality.

Take a look back at your high school years. I bet your friends had a set of unwritten rules to live by. They had certain understandings about whether it was acceptable or unacceptable to drink, smoke, have sex, go to parties, or listen to certain types of music. Even if you're a follower of Jesus, there's a good chance you had friends with different opinions on some of these issues. Maybe you chose to become friends with some people (and avoided others) based on the moral choices they made. Am I right?

If you're a follower of Jesus, your moral standards should be rooted in him. Christian morality is centered on Jesus Christ and Scripture. Thus, the standard for our conduct isn't based on popular opinion, but on the life of Jesus. Our choices should line up with what Jesus thinks.

Jesus came to earth to bring life, not death. He came to bring a life that is full, healthy, exciting, and joyful. It's called "overflowing" or "abundant" life (John 10:10). So the big question you need to ask yourself as you head toward adulthood is, "Are my choices headed toward overflowing life as Jesus described it?"

> When in doubt, I look to Scripture, but most of the time I know when things are right and wrong. I don't mind waiting a decade for the right guy, and I don't mind telling all the wrong ones "no." It's how I've always been, and I hope that resilience stays the same as I go on to college. —Shae, 18

Thinking Like Jesus

If we want our moral compass centered on Jesus, we need to change our way of thinking. Paul told the church at Philippi, "In your relationships with one another, have the same attitude of mind Christ Jesus had" (Philippians 2:5). In other words we need to do our best to think like Jesus.

If we can figure out what Jesus would say about a given situation before we act or speak, we're in great shape. Let's put this to the test:

What would Jesus think...

...about deciding to make out with someone you just met?

...about telling a "little white lie" to protect a friend?

...about having friends over for a drinking party when your parents are away?

...about stealing the final exam for a class you're taking, throwing it out the window, and picking it up after school so you ace the exam? (A high school friend of mine did this!)

These are all real life situations you or a friend might face. I know they're focused on the "negative" side of Christian morality, but it's important to decide ahead of time what we would do based on what Jesus would think. But the questions don't apply only to the "don'ts." We might also ask these questions:

What would Jesus think...

...about staying after school to help your shop teacher clean up and store equipment?

...about giving money to help a classmate who can't afford to buy lunch?

...about taking a short-term mission trip to help build houses in a poor community?

...about a couple making a commitment not to have sex before marriage?

I think Jesus would be pleased if you acted positively on these scenarios. This is where the rubber meets the road, when you graduate and become a mature, Christ-following adult.

A lot of the moral issues we face today are directly addressed by the Bible, but some questions are not. Still, I believe trying to think like Jesus really helps with even issues the Bible doesn't directly address. I believe our pursuing the Jesus of the Bible makes all the difference in how we look at the world. This pursuit isn't just a one-time event, but a daily commitment. As you do this your thinking will become more like the mind of Christ, and the lines of morality will become clearer.

Paul reminds us that Jesus is "the image of the invisible God, the firstborn of all creation," the One through whom "all things were created" (Colossians 1:15-16). Through Jesus, God came to Earth in human form. And through Jesus' death on the cross, we've been reconciled with God (1:20).

Have you ever wished you could see God? Maybe you think, *If he'd just appear in my bedroom one time, it would make a difference.* Well, God has appeared in our world, and his name is Jesus. Why did he? To bring people to himself; for his glory, honor, and delight. The cross brings life. The cross brings the lines of morality to our everyday lives through the guidance of the Spirit, who lives inside of every follower of Jesus.

> *A good way for me to stick to being morally pure is to ask myself (no matter how cliché it may be), "If Jesus were standing right there, what would he think?" or "Would I be embarrassed if Jesus saw me doing this?"*
> —Jaclyn, 17

Defining Your Morals and Values

God doesn't leave us hanging; he guides us in our morality. The whole of Scripture directs us toward a moral, Spirit-filled, overflowing life (John 10:10, Galatians 6).

In Matthew 5-7, we find Jesus' greatest sermon, the Sermon on the Mount. These few chapters hidden away at the beginning of Matthew's Gospel are a sort of Christian "Declaration of Independence" that provide marching orders for those who want to be disciples of Jesus. In this sermon, Jesus focuses not just on the importance of our actions, but also on the motives of the heart that lead to action.

At the very beginning of this famous sermon are a series of statements called the Beatitudes (5:2-12). Jesus tells the gathered crowd that God's blessing is on those who are humble (the poor in spirit), tender (those who mourn), broken (the meek), godly (those who hunger and thirst for righteousness), forgiving (the merciful), clean (those who are pure in heart), and reconciling (the peacemakers). This isn't an easy list to live, and Jesus closes the list by acknowledging that people may insult or persecute those who live by these words. But he promises that those who base their actions in these characteristics will be blessed. These are incredible statements from the one who lived them out all the way to the cross. I suggest reading the rest of the Sermon on the Mount. It will guide your lines of morality as you transition to maturity.

> *I have to ask myself, "Why I am doing what I'm doing?" Am I selfishly pursuing after my own pleasures at any expense, or am I honestly doing things to love others? When what I'm doing turns into selfish obsession to get my own pleasures, morality has gone out the window.*
> —Ryan, 24

A Few Specifics: Honesty and Integrity

Let me get more specific for a minute. How important do you think honesty is? Is lying acceptable? Do your friends tend to lie? Are "little white lies" okay? Dishonesty has become the norm these days. How one determines whether it's okay to lie or not is based on individual circumstances, like protecting yourself or a friend. Instead of asking the question, "What would Jesus think of me lying?" we lie almost instinctively.

I've heard some young people say, "Everybody lies, and everybody knows that everybody lies." There's research to support that many teenagers and twentysomethings lie on a regular basis.[3] But when those same people are asked if they're honest, the answer is "Yes, I'm basically an honest person." Yet their actions often tell a different story.

As you head into adulthood, you'll be tempted to lie in small and big ways. Maybe you'll be asked about your past work experience in a job interview, and you'll wonder if you should exaggerate in hopes of getting the job you've always wanted. Maybe you'll be tempted to tell your parents your college grades are better than they really are. Maybe, when your boss asks you a question at work, you'll lie without even thinking about it and lose your job. Perhaps the consequences will never be so quick and direct, but I assure you, there will be consequences. In your pursuit of holiness, I encourage you to ask yourself before lying, "What would Jesus think of my lying in this moment?"

A couple of other temptation areas you'll wrestle with are integrity and trustworthiness. Have you or your friend ever cheated on a test? Maybe it was giving an answer to their friend during a final exam. Or maybe it was something that seems even more trivial, like fibbing in gym class about the number of pushups you did. According to national research, the rate of cheating among high school and college students is rising, though college students tend to cheat less than high school students according to some surveys.[4]

> *Morality is a BIG deal in my life. I think our culture looks at morality as a joke, but I take it very seriously. I see the consequences of making bad decisions.*
> —Candice, 17

Draw the line now. As you become an adult follower of Jesus, choose not to cheat in any form. Minor cheating now could morph into cheating on your taxes in the future. That's how sin works—

3 Dr. Chap Clark of Fuller Theological Seminary has done hands-on research among adolescents in this area, and it's documented in his book, *Hurt: Inside the World of Today's Teenagers* (Baker, 2004).
4 Clark, *Hurt*, 152.

you think you're in control of yourself, but sin's really in control of you. This is why Paul told the followers of Jesus at Colossae. "Do not lie to each other, since you have taken off your old self with its practices and have put on the new self, which is being renewed in the knowledge in the image of its Creator" (Colossians 3:9-11).

As a follower of Jesus, ask for God's helping in making moral choices rooted in honesty and integrity. Make the decision now to avoid lying or cheating in any form that would prevent you from making a smooth transition into becoming an adult who wholeheartedly loves Jesus.

Questions for the Journey

1. Brainstorm a list of the immoral actions you see in the world. How does this list make you feel?

2. How do you determine your lines of morality? What's your measuring stick?

3. Do you know friends who've lied or cheated in the last few months? How do you respond to this behavior? What can you do to stay away from falling into this trap?

4. What steps can you take to cultivate honest, encouraging relationships as you make the transition into the real world?

Web Resources

teensagainstporn.com

With the increase of pornographic temptations, this is a place where teenagers help other teens in the battle with pornography addiction, including accountability, articles, and resources.

teenhollywood.com
This is a site for teens and twentysomethings to check out and discuss the latest news in music, movies, and television. There is also a section where teens can write in and get advice.

Book Resources

The Purity Principle: God's Guardrails on Life's Dangerous Roads by Randy Alcorn (Multnomah Publishers, 2003).

Boundaries: When to Say Yes, When to Say No To Take Control of Your Life by Dr. Henry Cloud and Dr. John Townsend (Zondervan, 2008).

Intellectual and Ethical Development by William Perry (Rinehart and Winston, 1970).

Fundamentals of Ethics by John Finnis (Georgetown University Press, 1983).

CHAPTER 7
DIRECTION: YOUR CHOICE OF A MAJOR

It's okay not to know what you want to do right away! Value the advice and thoughts of your parents and friends, be flexible, and focus on God. —Rob, 26

The Black Hole

Every time my family goes to Sam's Club to shop, the kids ask my wife for a coin. (They know I never have any money.) I know where they're headed. There's this game where you drop a nickel in the slot and then get dizzy watching it go around. First, the coin makes long, wide circles at the top. I watch their eyes spin in circles, and I get light headed. Then the coin rolls around and around the bowl, each rotation becoming a little smaller. Finally the coin spirals down through an open hole in the bottom.

So how do you choose your direction? If you are a college student, how do select your academic specialty, better known as the dreaded major, knowing that it will shape your career possibilities?

This process looks a little like the coin game we talked about: You might think yourself in circles before you finally hone in on your center. As you wholeheartedly obey God and proactively look for his specific purpose for your life, as you explore different areas and interests and stay sensitive to God's leading, he'll draw you toward the center of his will for you. In the beginning you may feel like you're taking very long and broad rotations around your major, like an airplane circling an airport, stuck in a holding pattern as it prepares to land. That's the way it works. But over time, as you move toward the center, as you gravitate toward subjects and classes you enjoy, you'll find your direction.

Areas of Discovery

Whether you're in high school or early college, you already have interests that relate to your major-to-be. From the moment you were born, throughout elementary school and all the way through high school, God has been molding you into who you are. If you've surrendered your life to Jesus, and you're actively following after him today, the Holy Spirit lives in you and guides you to your purpose.

Choosing a major can be an important part of determining your future career path. Here are some things to help guide you as you circle, searching for your sweet spot in the center of God's will.

First, look to *Scripture*. God will use your growing relationship with Jesus and the study of Scripture to help you grow into the person he wants you to be. For example, as you read the letter to the Galatians you discover there are acts that lead to living a sinful life and acts that lead to living a fruitful life. Paul says the fruit of the Spirit is "love, joy, peace, patience, kindness, goodness, faithfulness, gentleness, and self-control" (5:19-26). After reading through this passage, you might find yourself confessing situations in which you've given into sinful behavior and asking God to help you live a fruitful life. Something supernatural happens in this experience of study. God begins to change your character and, in doing so, reveals to you who you are and what you're to do.

Second, look for *open doors*. These are opportunities and experiences that are right in front of you. In college, there are so many classes to choose from. You aren't expected to know what you're going to do with the rest of your life the day you bust out of the double doors. Your early college years are years of discovery. There are many general education classes you'll need to take to graduate, but you'll also have opportunities to take elective classes that let you explore different areas. The larger the university, the more classes you'll have to choose from.

In addition, look for opportunities to serve on or off campus. Getting paid is a bonus, but don't expect to make money during the discovery process. Keep your eyes and ears open for God's divine appointments. He wants to help you find the major and career direction that will best fit you and give you the greatest joy. Ask yourself, "What does the world need that's a good fit with my abilities and interests?" This question might direct you toward an area of study and a major.

Third, look to your *heart*. As you take classes, stay in tune with the Holy Spirit's guidance. Keep asking yourself questions: "Do I enjoy this class? What do I like and dislike? Could I see myself working in this field the rest of my life? If I could do anything I wanted for the rest of my life, what would it be?" Ask God to give you a peace about your decisions.

> *I had a major, went with it for a semester, and dropped it. Don't think you have to have your life all planned out when you're handed your high school diploma or GED. Many students change their major or transfer to a different school before they complete college.*
> —Gloria, 18

The path your heart reveals may surprise you. When I was growing up, I didn't like to read. My mom tried everything, but I always preferred being outside with a ball playing sports, like soccer, basketball, and tennis. In time, I began to enjoy reading as I found my areas of interest: theology and culture. You may find yourself drawn to something you didn't like at an earlier age.

Fourth, look to your *design*. Paul says that each of us is "God's workmanship created in Christ Jesus to do good works which he created in advance for us to do" (2:10). God has designed you to make a unique contribution in this world. With a consistent and growing relationship with Jesus, this design can be discovered.

As you step off the metro trains in the United Kingdom, you can hear a recorded voice reminding riders to "mind the gap" when stepping from train to the platform. Well, you need to stay alert and "mind the GAP"—your Gifts, Abilities, and Passions. God has designed each one of us with gifts, abilities, and passions ready to be discovered and used in his service. It's our responsibility to discover our spiritual gifts, natural abilities, and passions by serving in many areas.

Finally, look to your *church community* for affirmation. Don't underestimate the importance of having a local congregation of believers surrounding your life. As you head into the real world, you might be traveling a far distance from your home church. If that's the case, make sure you become involved in a congregation near your college. Get to know some people and begin to serve. Ask them what they think about your gifts, abilities, and passions. Chances are very good that, as you serve, you'll talk about areas that are important to you and fire you up. Your fellow church members could help you discover your major and future direction.

> *My first shot at a major was a combination of strengths that I'd seen evident in my life in high school: leadership, math, organization, and service. It all went together for business.*
> —Deb, 28

Tips for Exploring Your Major

As you apply these tips above to discovering your major, consider some additional questions.[5] Take some time with God and journal your answers.

1. What do you really enjoy doing? (You could spend all day doing this. You love it.)

2. What can you do better than most people? (This isn't a prideful thing; just be honest.)

3. What would those who know you best say your greatest strengths are? Ask them.

4. Of the following jobs listed here, which three are most appealing to you, and why? Accountant, fireman, computer programmer, nurse, mechanic, surgeon, farmer, lawyer, architect, flight attendant, astronomer, business executive, professor, teacher, policeman, engineer, scientist, dentist, paleontologist, statistician, psychiatrist, entrepreneur, salesman, therapist, doctor, contractor, real estate developer, writer, musician, pastor, youth pastor, missionary, actor/actress, yodeler, zoologist, politician, store owner, stockbroker, pilot, pharmacist, consultant.

5. What did you enjoy most about high school? ("Nothing" is not an answer.)

6. If money weren't an obstacle, what would you spend your time doing? (Again, doing "nothing" is not an answer.)

7. If you could be famous for something, what would your accomplishment be?

8. What needs do you see in the world that you'd like to help meet?

5 These questions were adapted from Sean Covey's *The Six Most Important Decisions You'll Ever Make* (Fireside, 2006).

9. What's God asking you to do?

10. Is there something you've always felt you should do with your life, but didn't have the courage to do?

These questions can lead you toward your major and other life goals. You don't have to have it all figured out by tomorrow, but you can't steer a parked car, either. Start the car. Start serving. Start listening to God's voice. Start paying attention to his movements and the relationships he places in your life.

Timothy's "Major"

Timothy was a young man who traveled with Paul on missionary journeys and sometimes stayed behind when Paul left to work with other churches. Some scholars believe Paul might've led Timothy to Christ. In fact, Paul's last two letters before he died were written to Timothy.

Paul's first letter to Timothy is filled with all kinds of good advice. The aging apostle urged his young friend to "flee" evil and "pursue righteousness, godliness, faith, love, endurance and gentleness" (1 Timothy 6:11). In other words, Paul told Timothy to run away from bad stuff and run at good stuff. Then he urged Timothy, "Fight the good fight of the faith. Take hold of the eternal life to which you were called when you made your good confession in the presence of many witnesses" (6:12). That's good advice for Timothy and every follower of Christ.

Obviously you want to try and figure out what God wants you to do. If that isn't clear when you enter college, pick something you enjoy. Most people change their majors a couple times throughout their college career, so it's not the end of the world if you want to change it after your first semester. However, be aware that some programs are a lot more rigid than others (nursing, education, etc.), and you could add significant time and money if you change too often. —Adam, 23

Paul offered similar words of challenge in his second letter to Timothy: "But as for you, continue in what you have learned and have become convinced of, because you know those from whom you learned it" (2 Timothy 3:14). Paul told Timothy to follow Jesus for the long haul.

But it's in chapter four that Paul gives Timothy his calling. He tells him to "preach the Word" and to "do the work of an evangelist" (2 Timothy 4:1-5). This was Timothy's major; he was to teach the world about Jesus Christ. If there were seminaries or Bible colleges in his day, Timothy might have attended one for training. Paul helped Timothy discover a major that connected to his passions, gifting, natural talents, and desires.

You need a "Paul" or two who will help you as you take this journey of discovering your major. As Timothy went through a process of discovering the direction God was leading him in, he needed people willing to walk with him. The same is true for you. Don't try to go it alone.

Questions for the Journey

1. As you look ahead to college, are you excited about discovering your major? Or are you stressed?

2. What are the top five things you like to do? How could these be connected to your major and life calling?

3. What steps can you take to help discover your major?

Web Resources

ctlibrary.com/rq

Re:generation quarterly equips the next generation to transform their world.

interviewtips.org

> This is a good site for everything you need to know walking into and out of a successful job interview.

collegeboard.com/csearch/majors_careers/profiles/index.html

> This site has everything for planning and attending college, as well as lists of colleges based on career choices.

Book Resources

Congratulations...You're Gifted! Discovering Your God-Given Shape to Make a Difference in the World by Doug Fields and Erik Rees (Zondervan, 2008).

Guide to College Majors by The Princeton Review (Random House, most recent edition)

Purpose Driven Life: What on Earth Am I Here For? by Rick Warren (Zondervan, 2002).

Holy Discontent by Bill Hybels (Zondervan, 2007).

CHAPTER 8
LEARNING: YOUR CHOICES IN THE CLASSROOM

*Please pray I can maintain a Christlikeness in the university setting;
there is so much disbelief. People say they're not religious, but I
see they believe in themselves. The second day of geology class, a
student tried to argue that creationism is true and the class mocked
him. I nudged him and told him the timing was not right. The
professor said, "This is a science class, not a philosophy class." Later
I asked the professor, "If it's not a philosophy class, then why do you
believe in science?" He didn't have anything to say. I haven't been
that nervous for a long time. I really need some ideas or input on
how to live for Jesus in the college classroom. —Jonathan, 22*

College Class Confrontation

The quote above was taken from an email I received from a friend
who was wrestling with the college-classroom experience. He wrote
to ask for prayer and encouragement, and I asked if he'd let me
share the quote in this book. Why? It reveals the kind of classroom
challenges you can experience in a secular university environment.

My friend Jonathan has it right: We all believe in someone or something. Depending on where you go to school, you may find yourself surrounded by professors and other students who will support and encourage you in your faith in Jesus, or you may feel like your beliefs are constantly being challenged. Either way, if you're a follower of Jesus who wants to make a difference at your college, this section is for you.

Wisdom 101

Everything starts in your mind. First Corinthians 8:1-2 says, "We know that 'We all possess knowledge.' But knowledge puffs up while love builds up. Those who think they know something do not yet know as they ought to know." Our actions consciously or subconsciously start in our minds. Whether we're choosing to do wrong or right, it's our brain that's first in play.

College can be a wonderful place on so many levels, but it's a place where knowing what you believe is very important. When you come to know the real Jesus, your mind has a different master teacher. Paul tells us we get a brand new way of thinking when we become a follower of Jesus. He says, "Do not conform to the pattern of this world, but be transformed by the renewing of your mind. Then you will be able to test and approve what God's will is—his good, pleasing and perfect will" (Romans 12:2). This renewal of our minds starts with Jesus. Since Jesus is the same yesterday, today, and forever, we can depend on him for all wisdom and understanding (Hebrews 13:8-9). When you become a follower of Jesus, he's your pathway to true wisdom.

Proverbs tells us, "The fear of the Lord is the beginning of wisdom, and knowledge of the Holy One is understanding" (Proverbs 9:10). So wisdom starts with a healthy fear of God. What does this really mean? The fear this verse speaks of isn't a horror movie kind of fear; rather, we should be in *awe* of God. The God of the universe is *awesome*. Understanding this is where true wisdom starts.

Good Judgment

In college you'll need to practice good judgment. This takes wisdom, or discernment. When your English professor suggests you can never really know what an author meant by certain words, this should disturb your discernment radar. You begin to wonder: *Does that make sense? If I can't ever know what someone really means, how do I know what this professor means when she speaks?* If your science professor says the material world is all that's out there, that what you can see, taste, touch, smell, and hear is it, you think to yourself, *Science says there was a beginning to the universe, and if there was a beginning, then there had to be a Creator of it all.* You might have a literature prof who views the Bible as just another book, or even a religion professor who see the Bible as a purely human work. But then you begin to think about verses you've studied that speak to the Scriptures being God-inspired and Spirit-guided, like 2 Timothy 3:16 and 2 Peter 1:20-21.

Your discernment must be based on your growing relationship with God, your consistent study of Scripture, and the promise of the Holy Spirit guiding you to truth. Ask God to guide you. Stay on your toes. Listen closely to what your professors say and learn from them, but understand that you don't have to believe everything they say.

Some students who've given their lives to Jesus find themselves at a crossroads of belief in certain college classrooms. Consider Susan, a young Christian who only recently made a decision to follow Jesus. She walks into her freshman philosophy class and encounters a professor who says the philosophy of the Bible is ignorant compared to other human philosophies. He seems to think human authority is

Pray for wisdom, asking God to show you the right path. —David, 18

more important than divine authority. Susan thinks to herself, *This professor is a tremendously intelligent person with a doctorate from an Ivy League university. He wrote the textbook that cost me an arm and leg to buy. Maybe he's right. I'm not sure I like everything in the Bible. Maybe I'd be better off as my own boss.*

This is when a crisis of belief comes at Susan like a ton of bricks. She's on her own now. She has total freedom from her parents and other authority figures. She feels she can't believe in both God's wisdom and her own wisdom. Worse yet, she feels she can't believe in both philosophy and Scripture. It's either this way or that. She wonders, *Is Jesus my Lord, or am I in charge?* As a result, Susan concludes that her philosophy professor is right. Her values are more important than God's.

This is a real situation that you may encounter in college, but it doesn't have to be a crisis of faith. Use your discernment in the classroom. Remember, just because many of your professors have doctorates and book credits and are showing you "evidence" in class doesn't mean everything they say is true. Ask God to give you his wisdom and discernment to know the truth. Don't throw away your faith in Jesus because one professor says something that contradicts something you've learned from a parent or pastor.

> *Know what you believe. Don't challenge your professors' authority, but stand by your understanding of God.*
> —*Sally, 18*

The reality is all truth is God's truth. Jesus says, "I am the way, the truth and the life..." (John 14:6). Each of your professors is made by God in God's image. Even if they're not followers of Christ, they're able to speak God's truth. Your physics professor might explain the theory of gravity. Scripture doesn't explain gravity in scientific terms, but it's still a truth: God set up the universe and created gravity. The important thing is to start with the truth of Scripture and let God guide you into the full truth. Default to God and his Word over your professors' words—or your own!

> *I test everything against what I see in the Bible and in God's character and through prayer.*
> —Ryan, 24

In college (and throughout your life), it's important to surround yourself with smart and discerning people who possess depth of character and who love Jesus with all of their heart. These are people who might become mentors to you. (See chapter 12 on *Mentoring*). There are many Christians who've already walked the road you're walking. The issues you'll face in the college classroom are not new, and many people have been helped through these times by a community of intelligent Christ-followers. Martin Luther King Jr. said it best with the following words: "Intelligence plus character—that is the goal of a true education." A community of fellow disciples can help make sure your education is one that builds both intelligence and character.

Seven Steps to College Success

The first time you enter a college classroom you'll immediately notice the differences from a high school class. For one thing, class sizes can vary dramatically. You may have some highly specialized classes with a dozen students or less, but other courses may have hundreds of students packed into the same lecture hall. Whatever the class size, here are a few suggestions to help you succeed in the classroom:

1. Get a laptop and take it to class with you. Hopefully you took a typing class in high school. If you still have time, take it your senior year. I can't tell you how important it was for me to take a basic typing class. I was bored out of my mind, but it really paid off—today, I type on my computer all the time. You'll save time by typing your notes and organizing them later. Don't spend class time playing games or emailing.

2. Take good notes. Maybe you were able to get through high school without having to take notes, but in college, you'll have to learn to take effective notes. Listen carefully to what your professor

says, but don't try to write down every word. Ask yourself, *Is this important to the professor? Is it likely to be on an exam or useful for a paper or assignment?* If you can make friends with an upperclassman who took the class, you can ask them what your professor looks for in a good paper or what kinds of questions are on exams.

3. Take time after class to review your notes; this will save you time later. Instead of going back over your notes for the first time a day before the final exam, do little reviews after class. This will keep the information in your brain longer. Right before bed is another great time to review your notes. Your brain will spend time with these thoughts all night and you'll retain the information longer.

4. Make an effort to meet those you don't know in your class, especially those who sit near you. Most of us are creatures of habit, so you'll probably sit in the same area every class and so will those around you. Who knows, you might meet a great lifelong friend (or a future spouse)!

5. Sit in the front row (or at least near the front of the class). I know you think I'm crazy on this one, but you'll learn more and pay better attention. Instead of looking at the backs of a dozen (or more) heads in the rows in front of you, you're better off sitting closer to the one who grades your papers.

6. Turn off your cell phone. There's nothing more distracting than a cell phone ringing, vibrating, or being typed on. You'll miss something important. Your friends can wait, even if they are sitting in the same class.

7. Arrive early to class. Don't be the one who's trying to sneak in late—this won't sit well with your professor. You're paying to take these classes, so come early and get your money's worth!

> *There are a lot of college professors in the classroom who'll tell you everyone needs to figure out their own beliefs and everyone's beliefs are okay. This is a dangerous adventure if your core values aren't nailed down.*
> *—Adam, 23*

8. Don't check your brains at the classroom door. Be wise. Pay attention. Test everything. Is it from God, or from another source? Is it true or false? There are times when you need to memorize something just to make the professor happy or to spit back some facts on a test, but most of the time you need to be discerning. Enjoy this stretching, challenging, and joyful time as you make choices to follow Jesus into the college classroom and beyond.

Questions for the Journey

1. How do you think the college classroom will compare to your high school classroom?

2. How do you intend to grow in wisdom while you're in college?

3. What's your game plan for discerning truth from error in the classroom lectures and reading?

4. How will you go about finding a trusted, Jesus-following friend to test what you learn?

Web Resources

liveabove.com

Live Above is a great Christian site to find campus ministries, roommates, and other resources when heading to college.

collegefaith.org

College Faith is another good Christian site for resources on staying close to Jesus in college.

education-portal.com/articles/Studying_101:_Guide_to_Studying_in_College.html

This is a good site for everything college-related, particularly creating good study habits.

Book Resources

The Case for a Creator by Lee Strobel (Zondervan, 2004).

The Truth War by John McArthur (Thomas Nelson, 2007).

Ask Me Anything 2: More Provocative Answers for College Students by J. Budziszewski (NavPress, 2007).

How Now Shall We Live? by Chuck Colson (Tyndale, 2004).

CHAPTER 9
STRESS: YOUR CHOICES UNDER PRESSURE

My family life puts a lot of stress on me. My parents recently divorced and it took a huge toll on me. Life at home can get crazy, and sometimes I lose sight of God. Problems with and between my friends also stress me out. It seems there's always one problem or another, and it would just be nice to have some peace. —Jaclyn, 17

Pressure and Peace

If there's one thing that almost everyone in their late teens and twenties has in common, it's that six-letter word. I'll give you a hint: It starts with "s" and rhymes with *mess*. Do you know it? It's S-T-R-E-S-S.

According to a recent survey in *Advertising Age*, 41 percent of twentysomethings say they feel either quite a bit of pressure or almost more stress than they can bear. When I started to write this book, I sent out a questionnaire to more than 100 young people. I asked them what things in their lives were causing stress. Here are just a few of the responses:

- Money

- Jobs

- Housing

- School

- Relationships

- Disappointing my parents

- Not sleeping

- Sports

- Acceptance

- Picking the right friends

- Staying friends

- Sinning

- Trying to keep up with everything

- What will happen after high school

- Using my time wisely

- Being bored

- Myself

This list has kept me praying for those young people and all of you who are reading this book during this transitional time in your life. But I think it's the very last word on the list that most concerns me. When the pressure is on, when all those other areas are pushing in on you, it can be hard to look in the mirror and not be stressed at what you see. That's one of the reasons this book was written and why we began with a section on *Identity*. When you know who you are and what you believe, when you place your faith in Christ and foster intimacy with Jesus, the peace of God sits deep in your heart.

I take time to rest and relax by sitting on the couch, snuggling in a blanket while watching a good movie. Sometimes you need to just get away from all the hectic stuff in life. —Jodi, 15

That doesn't mean you'll never face times of stress and difficulty—you will. But because of your relationship with Jesus, peace will dwell in your heart. You'll have an inner confidence that God is in control of your life. That kind of deep peace with God offers you calmness and security that can sustain you regardless of the circumstances.

Good News

When I think about this kind of peace, I often reflect on a scene from Scripture that's usually connected to Christmas. Now maybe you're reading this book during the heat of the summer. If so, you might want to pause your reading and make yourself a cup of hot cocoa, just to get in the Christmas spirit. Go ahead, I'll wait....

Now go with me to a hillside where shepherds watch their sheep. Get into the shepherds' sandals for a few minutes. Feel the breeze on your face. Listen to the "baaaaaa's" of the sheep. Look down toward the city of Bethlehem nearby.

Then—POOF! Out of nowhere, an angel appears in front of you with a most surprising message: "Do not be afraid!" *Are you kidding?* you think. *Of course I'm afraid. You're an angel, and I don't see angels everyday. As a matter of fact, I've never seen an angel.* But the angel continues, "I bring you good news of great joy that will be for all the people. Today in the town of David a Savior has been born to you; he is the Messiah, the Lord. This will be a sign to you: You will find a baby wrapped in clothes and lying in a manger."

You and the other shepherds look at one another, wondering if you can really believe what you just saw and heard. *Amazing! What does this mean? The long-awaited Messiah has come. In that city? Really? The Messiah? The one who'll finally rescue all of us?*

Then, SLAM! BAM! Now a multitude (that's a lot) of angels appear and begin singing, "Glory to God in the highest heaven, and on earth, peace to those on whom his favor rests." It gets even better. Peace has come. The angels leave, you pick your jaw up off the ground, grab your crook, and head for Bethlehem to see the Messiah—the Prince of Peace. When you finally get there and see Jesus, you're so astonished that you run out the door to tell everyone (Luke 2:8-20)!

I think this familiar story, with its message of peace, has some lessons we can use year-round to tackle the stress in our lives.

First, realize that peace is a gift from God. The angels announced this good news to the shepherds. The peace announcement has been given to you, too. The coming of the Messiah offers the promise of inner peace to every human, as well as an end to warring between nations.

Second, the story tells us peace should be pursued with passion. The shepherds didn't sit around after the angelic rock concert and say, "Well, that was nice, but I wish they'd had a little more drum." No, they hurried off to see the Savior. We can't sit and whine in our stress. The writer of Psalms says it clearly: "Seek peace and pursue it" (Psalm 34:14).

> Rest and relaxation are so important. There are times when I just need to be by myself and escape into nature. At other times, being with others and having a great laugh is enough to bring life back into my worn-out body.
> —Ryan, 24

Third, it's the Messiah who offers peace. When the shepherds arrived at the side of the cradle, looked into baby Jesus' eyes, and touched his fragile hands, I imagine their hearts melted. I think they surrendered to the Prince of Peace in that moment. We also need to make peace with the Messiah on an ongoing basis. Scripture tells us that we have peace with God through Jesus (Romans 5:1).

Fourth, the story tells us that this peace is not meant for us alone, but must be passed on to the planet. You're probably not the only one stressed-out about the circumstances of life. There are others whose situations are worse that yours. As a matter of fact, there are many who face the stress in their own lives without Jesus to help them through the tough times. They don't know the Prince of Peace. It's our job to partner with God and tell them this story. The shepherds were the first evangelists on the planet. They ran off to tell the world about Jesus. We should, too.

Fifth, this peace is something worth praising God about. The shepherds gave us a model: They returned to glorify God and praise Jesus for his birth. They remained in awe of this whole event. Worship has a way of helping us cope with the stress around us. When you're dealing with difficulty, work up the courage to sing new songs to the Lord. Make some joyful noise to the King of Kings.

> *I just hang out with my Christian friends and I use that time to get relaxed and refocused.*
> —Suzie, 18

Handling Depression

What if there's more to this stress? It's no secret that high school and the years that follow are a time when many people fall into depression. According to *www.teenhealthandwellnness.com*, suicide is the third leading cause of death among people ages 15 to 24 in the United States. Depression is a very serious problem. Don't be fooled: Even those who love Jesus can struggle with depression.

Maybe you feel like your problems are so overwhelming that you don't know what to do. Perhaps you think you're stupid for even feeling this way. There is hope—but you can't do it alone.

Many who are in the dark hole of depression choose to keep it to themselves, believing they can fight their way through it alone. They're trying to build their own life preservers even as they feel themselves drowning in the open sea. This is no time to be silent. This is the time to yell for help! Go. Run. Hurry. Choose a close and trusted friend, pastor, brother, sister, mom, dad, step-mom, step-dad, grandparent, professor, physician, coach, teacher, or counselor. And if the first person you tell doesn't take you seriously, keep searching until you've found a trusted friend who can help.

Don't worry about looking dumb or feeling too needy. We were built for community and connection with others. And remember: Jesus will always be there with you, even as you walk through this valley of death. Jesus walked through the same valley just hours before he was nailed to the cross for our sins (Luke 22:39-46). There's good news: If there's a valley, there must be a mountaintop. No matter how difficult it might seem, victory is yours through Jesus Christ who conquered death.

> I spend alone-time with God to get refreshed by enjoying God's creation.
> —Justine, 17

A Place of Tranquility

In 1969 astronauts landed on the moon for the first time. (I know—that was before you were born. In fact, it was before I was born, too.) After the Eagle landed on the moon, the astronauts set up what would be called Tranquility Base. It was an ironic name for the site of such a daring and dangerous mission.

Did you know that when Neil Armstrong landed that spacecraft on the moon, he had less than a minute of fuel remaining? In fact, some scientists estimate there were only 11 seconds worth of fuel left! Eleven seconds! Can you believe it? And they performed that whole moon mission with less computer power than I have in my minivan! NASA seemed to be communicating a biblical principle: You can have peace in the midst of stress.

Oceanographers say that no matter how high the ocean waves might be at any particular moment, the sea is always tranquil and peaceful 20 feet below the surface. No matter how bad the storm rages on top of the ocean, the waters are calm down deep. The believer in Jesus finds peace in the same place—down deep! Shallow belief in Jesus leaves you anxious and fearful when the storms rise, but deep, stable faith in Jesus provides tranquility in the midst of severe and threatening storms.

One of the most important things you can do when you're feeling stressed is gain perspective. Take care of yourself. Go buy a grande carmel macchiato from Starbucks and drink it in a hammock. Take a chill pill. Exercise like crazy. Pray without ceasing. Run a lap. Play soft music. Take large, overwhelming tasks and break them into bite-sized pieces. Buy a punching bag. Find a hot tub. Light some candles. Say no to something. These are all good ideas. Try them.

On the other hand, there are some things you shouldn't do while attempting to deal with stress. If you're stressed, don't bite your fingernails, get drunk, do everything all at once, take pills, drive like crazy, eat a whole quart of ice cream, fill your calendar so full you can't breathe, punch your roommate (even if you say you're doing it "in Jesus' name"), play in the road, or put firecrackers in your mouth and light them. These aren't good ideas. Don't do them.

I want to end this chapter on a more serious note—and hopefully one that will give you some hope when the stress is real. Paul gave the Christians in Corinth (and all followers of Jesus) a great reminder, even when times get difficult: Do not lose heart. "We are hard pressed on every side, but not crushed; perplexed, but not in despair; persecuted, but not abandoned; struck down, but not destroyed" (2 Corinthians 4:8-9).

Let me put it another way: You might feel like a quarterback being rushed by a whole gang of linebackers, but you'll never be sacked. Every now and then you might feel like a rubber band stretched to your max, but you won't break. You might feel like a deer being pursued through the woods on a wintry day, but you'll never be hunted down. There are even times when you'll feel like a boxer being beaten, bruised, and thrown against a wall repeatedly, but you won't be knocked out.

Why? Because "we always carry around in our body the death of Jesus, so that the life of Jesus may also be revealed in our body" (2 Corinthians 4:10). We're like jars of clay (2 Corinthians 4:7)—fragile and breakable on the outside, but strong like iron on the inside because Jesus lives in us.

> When I'm alone, I can just belt out my praises or requests to God.
> —Haylee, 15

So we don't lose heart. We don't give up or give in to stress. We're maturing as we follow Jesus.

Questions for the Journey

1. What stresses you out?

2. Do you feel like your life is coming together or falling apart?

3. How has God used stressful moments to shape who you're becoming?

4. What are some habits you can develop to combat stress as you follow Jesus?

Web Resources

christianitytoday.com/teens

> This is the online version of *Campus Life,* a relevant, cutting-edge Christian magazine for teens. The site features articles from the current issue, complete past issues, message boards, and an offer for a free hard copy of the publication. Lots of links to other sites (advice, humor, reviews, resources, trends, and stats) make this valuable for teens, youth workers, and parents.

suite101.com/lesson.cfm/18867/2346

> This site has good tips for reducing stress in college and beyond. It also has other resources for the college student.

Book Resources

Freedom of Simplicity by Richard Foster (HarperCollins, 1998).

How to De-Stress Your Life by Gregory L. Jantz (Revell, 2008).

Prayer That Relieves Stress & Worry by Eddie Ensley (Contemplative Press, 2007).

PART THREE:

BELONGING – Where Do I Fit?

Belonging

Identity

You

Choices

Your brothers and sisters in Christ are your support group, your true friends. They'll stand with you no matter what, and they'll help bring you back if you ever fall away. They're your anchor, your life raft, your survival kit, part of your fit on earth; you can't make it through the hostile waters of life without them. They're invaluable. —Shae, 18

As you long for freedom from your parents, as you long to get out on your own, there's this voice inside you yelling, "Let me out of here! I'm my own person!" The world affirms this demand. From music to television to movies, the message gets repeated again and again: "It's all about you."

We've already talked about how important it is to discover your design, to realize the unique person God created you to be. But that doesn't mean you're meant to go it alone. You were designed for connection, for relationship with others. Jesus affirms the importance of connection over and over through all the "one another" ideas in his teachings: Love one another, serve one another, bear one another's burdens, forgive one another, and many more.

We all know we're connected to other stories: God's story and the stories of those around us. Whenever someone says, "Wow, it's a small world," we can be sure that person has just discovered another connection. We're pieces of an amazing puzzle that God has assembled.

Think of your friends—in high school, college, or on the job. You love them, care for them, and would probably die for them. You already understand the importance of these connections. You know we were made not just for individual stuff but for together stuff.

So you're looking for freedom but long for community. This is called *interdependence*. It can be a difficult tension inside you—a push and pull between "me" and "us." In this section, we'll walk through places of belonging, starting with parents and moving through the other key connections in your life. My prayer is that you'll discover new ways in which your relationships can help you become a fully mature, Jesus-following adult.

CHAPTER 10
FAMILY: YOUR FIT WITH PARENTS

Leaving home was a good thing for my relationship with my parents because I learned to value them more. It changes when you get older. You learn that your parents have desires and passions outside of you. I make it a point to know them and understand them. I'm starting to value so much my parents' advice and opinions, but I'm also learning that I'm a separate person and that I'm responsible for myself and for seeking the Lord's will in my life, not necessarily my mom's will. —Annie, 29

From Small to Big

When each one of my three children was born, there was a natural connection between my wife and the newborn child. It only makes sense. Laurie carried each of those kids in her body for nine months, gave birth to them, and nursed them. I don't mean to minimize the importance of dads or the strong connection between my kids and me. But it never surprised me that when baby Lillian, Levi, or Lara would begin to cry, the one they really seemed to want was their mommy. This is the way God's economy works.

But as a child grows and becomes a teenager, the attachment to parents changes. As kids grow more independent, they want to be in control. That often leads to conflict.

Think back to your last argument with your mom or dad. What was the argument about? What was it really about? It probably had something to do with you striving for independence and gaining control while doing your best to gain trust from them.

This is all natural. As you make the transition from adolescence into adulthood, you'll probably feel some tension from your mom and dad; it's difficult for them to let go. There's also tension on your end because you want them to let go. This can lead to a major tug-of-war. Understanding the tensions that surround this transition can help you understand some of your parents' "crazy" behavior.

Parenting is a tough job. Hopefully your parents have been able to do five things for you during your middle and high school years.[6]

First, I hope they've offered you understanding. This doesn't mean they always agreed with you or that they liked your words and actions all the time, but hopefully you knew that they loved you no matter what you did.

Second, I hope your parents have shown you compassion. There might have been times when your mom and dad wanted to get closer to you, but you felt suffocated and pulled away. It's natural for you to desire to be more independent, but that can be hard on your parents. Hopefully, they showed you real compassion as you sought greater independence.

Third, I hope your parents set boundaries for you so you had a safe balance between being fully alive and completely dead.

6 Chap and Dee Clark's book *Disconnected: Parenting Teens in a MySpace World* (Baker, 2007) has great insight into these tasks of parenting.

I hope they loved Jesus so much they wanted you to wholeheartedly love him, too, so they set up rules to help you move in the right direction. And I hope these boundaries were full of grace.

Fourth, I hope your parents offered you guidance. I hope your parents charted the course and helped you along your journey. This doesn't mean they should've chosen your college or decided whom you should marry, but I do hope they helped you find your direction and avoid rough terrain. Believe it or not, most parents have protected their children from many scrapes and bruises throughout their lives.

Finally, as you'll soon make this transition to college and beyond, I hope your parents have been able to let go. After being the ones who held your hand every time you crossed the street, I hope your parents have been able to release that hand, give you a hug, and let you set sail for adulthood. I hope they're your biggest fans for following after Jesus.

Understanding, compassion, boundaries, guidance, and letting go—those are five essential gifts parents can give their children. None of us is perfect, and I'm sure your parents haven't handled every situation exactly the way you wish they had. But if your parents have been able to offer you these things throughout most of your life, you've been blessed. Give them a call to say thanks.

What if They Didn't?

Unfortunately, not everyone has a healthy relationship with his or her parents. I'm not just talking about little conflicts that drive every teenager crazy. I'm talking about serious stuff.

I hope your relationship with your parents has been a healthy one. But if it hasn't, if you've been neglected, abandoned, or suffered from physical or sexual abuse, let me tell you how deeply sorry I am. It wasn't fair to you. It wasn't what God wanted for you. But there's hope. The psalmist offers encouragement for those who've been mistreated or abandoned when he declares God is the "father to the fatherless" (Psalm 68:5). God can make up the difference in your life even if one of your parents were not honoring God in their parenting of you.

Now let me say something else that might feel incredibly difficult if you're facing such a situation. For the sake of your own emotional and spiritual health, I would urge you to try to forgive your parents. I know that won't be easy—and maybe it can't happen immediately. But as you make the transition into adulthood, if your parents have fallen short in any of the tasks I mentioned earlier, offer them as much grace as you can. Don't hold it against them. Some of you might have a hard time with my words here, but God's desire is for forgiveness and health for you and your parents. God wants you to be whole, and I think the path to wholeness, as difficult as it may seem, is a journey of forgiveness, release, and love.

> I made an intentional shift in my relationship with my parents when I left high school. It's going to be different for everyone. I wouldn't recommend cutting your parents loose as soon as you graduate; you'll quickly find out all the things they've been doing for you that have made your life easier. —Adam, 23

Relationships Change

I probably don't need to tell you that relationships change over time (but I just did). You might not believe this today, but the people who've been your closest friends during the last three or four years may not be the people you stay closest to for the rest of your life. The friends you have in high school might not stay as close as they are now. I remember thinking that some of my high school buddies would be great friends for the rest of my life. Can I be honest? This may shock you, but nearly 20 years later, I don't even know where many of them are.

Your relationship with your parents will change, too. They will always be your mom and dad; but now, instead of them being the people who ground you for the weekend or allow you to go to the movies, they can become good friends. That's right: Your mom and dad can become close friends as you make this transition. If you don't believe me, listen to what a few well-known singers recently said about their changing relationships with their own parents:

> *My relationship with my parents improved after high school. The first time I was sick at college and called home I realized just how much I really missed my mom. I could see on my parents' faces how hard it was for them to move me in to my new college dorm room and then drive away. —Tammy, 28*

The reality is that I need her. She's smart and tough, and there's still so much for me to learn from her. But I need her in a different way now than I did when I was 16. —Singer Hilary Duff, speaking about her mother[7]

Now that I'm older, I get along with them better, but when I was a teenager—you know, you just fight. But of course I loved them.
—Singer Avril Lavigne, speaking about her relationship with her parents[8]

It's true: These strange people who've had so much to say about your life up to this point are also making a transition. They should be loosening up their grip and becoming friends with you, too.

From the time you were born, your relationship with your parents has been evolving—and it's in the process of changing again. As a child, you were very dependent on them. Today, you're becoming much less dependent, but you're still very connected.

---

7 *Cosmo Girl*, May 2007, 131.
8 *Cosmo Girl*, June/July 2007, 122.

Take some time to think about what a God-centered friendship with your mom and dad would look like. How could you bring approval and acceptance to them? How could you show your love to them as you near graduation and head into adulthood?

Honor Roll

Paul offered the church in Ephesus many tips for following after Jesus in households. Hidden away in a few verses are the expectations for children. Even though you're not a five-year-old anymore, you're still the child of your parents. Paul says, "Children, obey your parents in the Lord, for this is right. 'Honor your mother and father'—which is the first commandment with a promise—'so that it may go well with you and that you may enjoy long life on the earth'" (Ephesians 6:1-3).

Paul reminds us that back when God gave Moses the Ten Commandments, the commandment to honor our parents also included a reason: So that you'll have a long and rewarding life. In other words, if you honor your mom and dad, God's blessings of peace, love, joy, and the like will be all yours. There's a deep connection between your spiritual health and your honoring your parents.

But what does *honor* mean? Have you been on the honor roll at school? Does an honor guard sound familiar? Honor is displayed when you lift people up, love them, put them before yourself, celebrate them, and show the world you care for them.

Becoming a good friend to your parents starts with honoring them. Celebrate the fact that they changed your diapers, taught you to ride a bike, helped

I've maintained a good relationship with my parents by spending quality time with them. Sometimes I say no to friends who want to hang out so I can chill with my parents. You have to make time to talk with them and hang out if you want to keep a healthy relationship.
—Stephanie, 18

you with countless hours of homework, went to your sporting events, and maybe even helped you buy your first car (and covered the insurance). Think of all the great qualities they have—make a list.

But don't just keep these things to yourself. Plan a "date" with your mom and dad to tell them how valuable they are to you. If you're still in high school, plan this date before you leave for college. If you've already made the transition to college and beyond, plan the date for a time when you're home on break. After this first date, enjoy the benefits and blessings of more dates as you grow in your friendship with those who raised you.

Starting Fresh

> I don't keep anything bundled up inside with my parents, but I lay it all on the table so there are no regrets later.
> —Jodi, 15

Before I end this chapter, let me ask you a question: Do you know your parents? This might seem like a silly question, but think about it. It's quite possible that you went though your high school years feeling like your parents never really knew you. Am I right? There might have been days (and late nights) when you tried your best to express to your parents what was going on with you—your greatest needs, your biggest stresses, your deep faith in Jesus—but you weren't sure they understood. Maybe you felt like you and your parents were speaking two different languages.

Maybe your parents haven't always taken the quality and quantity of time necessary to really know you as an emerging adult. But let's put that aside for a minute and turn the table. Think about the question the other way around: Do you really know your parents?

Here's a series of questions to help you consider how well you know your mom and dad. Most of the questions can apply equally well to either parent. If you know the answer to these questions, that's awesome! If you don't, this might be a great list of things for you to talk about on your upcoming date with them.[9]

What color are your mom's eyes?

What is your dad's favorite thing to do?

What would your parents say is the nicest thing you could do for them?

If your mom and dad had all the time and money in the world, what would they spend their time doing?

What are their views on marriage?

What do your mom and dad think about Jesus?

What is your dad's greatest unfulfilled dream?

What place in the world would your mom most like to visit?

What was your dad's first full time job?

What does your mom remember about the major world events she's lived through?

Where did your parents first meet?

Who's your dad's closest friend?

What's your mom's favorite kind of music?

What were their favorite television shows when they were children?

---

9 This list of questions was adapted from Sean Covey's *The Six Most Important Decisions You'll Ever Make* (Fireside, 2006).

Whom did your parents vote for in the last election? Why?

Does your dad fill up the car's gas tank when it's half-empty or wait until the last possible moment?

What's your mom's favorite place to eat out?

How did you do? These questions sound like questions you'd ask on a first date. No matter how well you did on this exercise, keep striving to know your parents better and really discover what it means to become adult friends with them. This new relationship has the potential to challenge you, stretch you, and take you deeper with Jesus. Take advantage of building beautiful friendships with your parents.

Questions for the Journey

1. How is your relationship with your parents today? What are some areas in which it could improve?

2. How will your parents and family feel about your transition to college and beyond? What will be the most difficult aspect for them?

3. How do you feel about leaving home?

4. In what practical ways can you honor your parents?

Web Resources

nacacnet.org/MemberPortal/News/StepsNewsletter/

This is a good site for tips on understanding and maintaining a healthy relationship with parents as students transition off to college.

*collegeuniversity.suite101.com/article.cfm/college_students_
and_parents*

> This is a good site and article on maintaining peace and health between parents and college students.

Book Resources

The Peacemaker: Student Edition by Ken Sande and Kevin Johnson (Baker, 2008).

Fatherless America by David Blankenhorn (HarperCollins, 1996).

Everything Twentys by Paul Turner (Tyndale House, 1996).

CHAPTER 11
COMPANIONS: YOUR FIT WITH FRIENDS

A good friend is a person who is there with you when it's good and when things go bad. They are someone who will help you grow in Christ and care enough about you to tell you when you shouldn't be doing something. —Stephanie, 18

The Purple Dinosaur

Barney drives me crazy. You know who I'm talking about: The purple dinosaur on PBS. (Or is he a lizard?) For some odd reason children seem mesmerized by this guy in a big purple suit and his dance moves. But I don't get it.

I was introduced to this creature—part giant stuffed animal, part purple pillow—back when my oldest nephew was a young child. He's in college now—and to my amazement, *Barney & Friends* is still incredibly popular with little kids. Over the years countless children (including mine, until we banned Barney from our house) have sat in front of the TV screen spellbound, or sung and danced along with

Barney and his not-so-purple pals. Maybe the songs on the show (like "Clean up... clean up...") have a positive message, but whenever I hear them I just want to yell, "Stop watching! This isn't good for your health!"

But there's another Barney who's very real, and his ideas about friendship are very good for your spiritual health. His full name was "Barney...bas"—Barnabas. And like many other characters in the Bible, his name summed up who he was. The name Barnabas means *encourager*—and that's exactly what Barnabas was. He came alongside the apostle Paul with unconditional love and support. He was a good friend. Barnabas introduced the rest of the disciples to Paul because he believed in him. Difficult times came for Paul, but Barnabas represented, defended, and supported him in the midst of criticism. That's what good friends do.

There are many other scriptural examples of deep friendships, such as Jonathan and David or Ruth and Naomi. Ruth's care and commitment to Naomi was so deep that she once said, "Where you go I will go, and where you stay I will stay. Your people will be my people and your God my God" (Ruth 1:16). And Jonathan was so loyal that he protected David even when Jonathan's own father, King Saul, wanted David killed. The Bible says "Jonathan became one in spirit with David and loved him as himself" (1 Samuel 18:1). I think we all long for this kind of deep friendship—even if we're not used to talking that way. (Don't worry, guys: I'm sure they high-fived each other at times.)

I have a handful of very close friends. They're people who share my beliefs and make it a point to understand and care about my passions. These people are my lifeblood and I share with them, not only because it blesses me, but also because it blesses them. I value very much their opinions. I also have friends in my life who are social friends, who I hang out with and have just dumb conversation with. We laugh and have fun, but there's not much depth to them; we just have a lot in common. Then there are friends that I'm close to, but only because I know a lot about what's going on in their life. These are people that don't take a vested interest in me, but I know I'm in their life, perhaps to enrich them or pray for them. This works for me because I have people at the other end of the spectrum enriching me.
—Lori, 29

Facts about Friends

Long ago the Greek philosopher Aristotle said, "Without friends no one would choose to live." I think he's right on the money. Christ is the center of our lives, but good friendships are essential for the mature, Jesus-following adult. We were built for community—that's why God didn't leave Adam alone in the garden for long. First there was Adam, then Eve, and humans continued to reproduce. Need I say more?

> *A good friend is someone who lets me be vulnerable but someone who's also willing to be vulnerable with me. A good friend is someone who prays, listens, cries, challenges, and just stays silent. A good friend knows when you're operating out of hurt and desires to bring you home.*
> *—Sara, 29*

So what does it mean to be a good friend? Here are five suggestions to help keep your friendships healthy and strong as you follow Jesus:

1. Friends provide a shield. They don't leave you vulnerable. To be a good friend involves some healthy and Godly protection. Friends look out for each other. They keep each other out of danger and hold each other accountable. Friends have each other's backs.

2. Friends are faithful. A good friend doesn't run away when times get tough. Friends say things like, "I'm here for you no matter what." If a difficult and stressful event happens in your friendship, you stay in the fight (or discussion). Friends don't walk away.

3. Friends tell the truth. They don't lie or fake it. Telling the truth requires wisdom and courage. The truth needs to be told at the right time, in the right way, and to the right people. We can't run from it even if it's hard. If you love your friend, you'll be willing to tell the truth even when it's difficult.

4. Friends don't point fingers. Good friends ask questions; they don't place blame. If you're selfless, thinking of your friend as better than yourself, you won't accuse him of anything. Ask

questions of clarity, but don't point fingers. Friends don't draw conclusions until they have all the facts.

> A good friend is someone who I can share anything with and not be written off. A good friend doesn't ditch me for an activity or relationship.
> —Joe, 22

    5. Friends make the extra effort. They're intentional about making the first move toward reconciliation. They value the other more than themselves. They love with patience and care, as Paul explained to the Corinthian church (1 Corinthians 13).

Types of Friends

All of us intuitively know there are different types of friends. Some people have more friends than others (especially on Facebook), but not all our friends are on the same level of connection. Your friends might include both the woman at the grocery-store checkout that you say *hi* to once a week as well as the person you've known all your life and share your deepest secrets with. It's important to be aware of what stage your various friendships are in so you treat them with the proper amount of intimacy.

> My closest friends are the ones that I can share with on a spiritual level. They'll listen to me in my darkest, dirtiest moments and still be my friend. They're the ones I know I can call at any time, having full confidence they'll make time for me. I know I can call my best friend, Ryan, and tell him I need a place to stay for the weekend and he would make it happen. These kinds of friends are usually not made over night, but over a good amount of time.
> —Sam, 23

    There are people you meet at the mall or at the movies. These are people you happen to stumble across who don't influence your life very much. You might run into one such friend some evening and not see him again for months. But the funny thing about God is that he'll sometimes take a casual friend like this and, over time, turn him or her into a person you would die for. Just pay attention and stay alert to God's movement.

There are also friends you hang with. As you move from high school to college or a career, your friendships will change. The people you hung with in high school might feel more distant when you no longer see them everyday. But you'll develop new connections with people you feel safe with. Give these friends permission to speak into your life when you're high and low.

Then there's a smaller group of friends you really trust. When you have secrets to tell, this is the group you express them to. The closer you get to one another, the more vulnerable you are with them. The more you care about them, the more potential there is to be hurt by them. This is the group you laugh the hardest with and weep the longest with. There is deep trust.

Finally, over the course of your life you might have a few special friends with whom you feel closest. You'd do anything for these people. These friends believe in you and you believe in them. Nothing can get in the way of your love for these people. They're like food and air to your soul. Go further with them. Pray longer with and for them. Keep confidential things between you and these friends. These friends are precious—so love, foster trust with, and believe in them.

Friendship was God's design. If it's true that we all have a hole in our hearts that only God can fill, there are also human-sized holes that need to be filled. We only have so much time, energy, and room for friendships. Choose your friends wisely and you'll reap huge rewards.

> A good friend is someone who knows my heart, dreams, and passions. They also know my struggles and failures, yet love me and accept me completely, both good and bad. —Ryan, 24

Handling Conflict

Sometimes you'll experience conflict in your friendships. If you don't ever have conflict in your friendships, you don't have friends. Friends care enough to confront one another, and they care enough to be hurt by one another.

Learning how to handle conflict is essential. If not handled properly, conflict can deeply damage a person or relationship. Some people actually enjoy conflict (at least initially) while others run from it like they'd flee a burning home. Which way do you respond to conflict? Do you fight or take flight? Do you become aggressive or retreat? Do you demand it be resolved right now or hide your feelings like nothing happened? Understanding your own reactions in the first step to facing conflict.

> The closest friends would be the ones that I can tell anything to, trust with everything, and know that they'll have my back no matter what. The closer friends would be the ones that I have a good relationship with, but I may not always tell them everything on my mind or trust them with certain things. The close friends would be ones that I enjoy being around, but I probably won't tell them much and I can't be around them all the time.
> —Jaclyn, 17

Next, you need to understand the person you're in conflict with. Find a time to address the conflict with them face-to-face. Be willing to give each other time and space to cool down, collect your thoughts, and pray. Then, with mutual love and respect, pray and talk it out. Use "I felt" statements to talk about your own experience of the situation, not accusing "you" statements that criticize or place blame. Once you've discussed the problem and worked it out, decide (out loud) to forgive one another and put it behind you. This is hard, but keep practicing. Over time, this will help you grow closer to one another and God.

There's no single, universal formula for conflict resolution. Matthew 18 suggests some principles to follow when sin is clearly involved, but often the question of whether someone has sinned is part of the conflict. Of course, much conflict comes from pride, jealousy, envy, selfishness, and desire for control—and God is not honored by these motivations.

Always ask yourself, "What am I learning about myself in this conflict?" Stay humble and teachable. This will get you well on your way to developing deeper friendships and growing in your relationship with Jesus.

Questions for the Journey

1. What you are the qualities of a good friend?

2. How have you been a good friend to others?

3. How is your relationship with God like a friendship?

4. When difficult times come, who will walk beside you as you make this transition?

Web Resources

readthetattoo.com

Begun in 1994 with a small group of teen writers in Bristol, Connecticut, *The Tattoo* has grown into a widely respected online teen newspaper with writers from around the world. The site is filled with articles on every topic of interest to teenagers.

facebook.com

I am sure you're aware of social networking sites that can help you stay connected with friends and family. If you haven't already, you might as well sign up for Facebook—many twentysomethings have done so already. Warning: Do not become "friends" with everyone; protect yourself by limiting access to your profile to people you know well.

Book Resources

Wisdom On...Friends, Dating, & Relationships by Mark Matlock (Zondervan, 2008).

Friendship by Robert Cummins (St. Mary's Press, 2004).

Personal Notes to the Graduate by Laurie Beth Jones (Thomas Nelson, 2006).

CHAPTER 12
MENTORING: YOUR FIT WITH PEOPLE

I want to find a mentor who knows Christ and Scripture, who has wisdom, and who is trustworthy. —Annabel, 15

The Need for Mentors

Everywhere I go to speak and teach, I hear high school students and young adults asking, "Where is the older generation of Christians who should be pouring their lives into us? Where are the folks who can model what it means to be a mature adult follower of Christ?" These people are out there. Instead of wondering why they haven't found you, go out and find them! It's your responsibility to seek out the wisdom of those who've traveled the road of faith before you.

Let's call these people who are just a little further along in their journeys with Jesus *mentors*. They come in all shapes and sizes. The reason you pursue a mentor is because you see something in them that you want to imitate. Maybe it's the way they approach career, family, or ministry. Perhaps their integrity, character, or skills are attractive. As they imitate (or *mime*) the words and actions of Jesus, you want to imitate their words and actions.

Paul invited the church to follow his example even as he followed the example of Christ (1 Corinthians 4:16, 1 Thessalonians 1:6). We should do the same in our own efforts to follow Jesus—look to Paul and the mentors we find around us.

What Mentors Are—and Aren't

All of us need someone in life who's spiritually running ahead of us, who's been following Jesus a little longer. We need role models who can help us evaluate our feelings, thoughts, habits, motives, schedules, and goals.

This might sound scary or intimidating. You might be thinking, *Are you asking me to share my whole life with someone?* Maybe—that all depends on the relationship you establish with your mentor. Ideally, there's a transparency and depth to the relationship that allows you both to share the triumphs and struggles of your lives.

Before we think any further about finding a mentor, let me tell you what you're not looking for in a potential mentor. Mentors aren't perfect. They make mistakes, so don't be disillusioned when they fail. Mentors aren't there to help you gain fame and fortune. And they aren't superheroes: The person you are looking for isn't Superman or Wonder Woman.

A good mentor is human just like you, but a little further along in his or her spiritual maturity and life experience. I like the way my friend Eddie (in his 20s) described what he's looking for in a mentor:

> A good mentor is someone with more life experience than me, someone my same gender, someone who is more spiritually mature than me, someone who has a desire to

> *A mentor is someone who loves God with all their heart, has their head on straight, and knows what they're looking for. They don't settle and don't give up. —Candice, 17*

see me grow and become more mature than I am. A mentor is someone I trust my life with, a person I know I can get good advice from.

Mentors are mature friends, more like a beloved aunt or uncle than a strict father or mother. A good mentor will celebrate your strengths and allow you to share your weaknesses without condemnation. Mentors are rare individuals who can weep with us, teach us, correct us when necessary, love us deeply, see our greatest potential, and never give up on us. This is the type of person you need in your life.

Here are a few more characteristics I would look for in a mentor:

Look for a *servant*. This person needs to be able to give of themselves to others because they understand that Jesus came to serve. This might mean they give of their wisdom, resources, and time.

Look for someone who's *loyal*. You need someone who sees a commitment to you as part of his or her life and ministry. Talk about this with them. Ask them, "How important is this relationship to you?" You need them to be trustworthy and reliable.

Look for a mentor who is *authentic*. In a world full of fake people on stages and movie screens, you need a mentor who's real—someone who's as genuine as they seem. You don't want someone who's one kind of person on stage but another when the spotlights aren't on. You want someone who'll be open with you, admit mistakes, get excited about your successes, and show a transparent genuineness.

Look for someone who's *honest*. You need a mentor who will look at you objectively and willingly speak truth about your weaknesses and strengths. As you grow into a spiritually mature adult, you need honest and open mentors around you. (And when they tell you the truth, you shouldn't get defensive—you need to remain teachable.)

To sum it up, the best mentors are people who are pursuing God with everything they have and want to help others do so, too. Look for their godly character. Watch how they treat people with their words and actions. Don't look for perfection but brokenness and humility. They should remind you of Jesus.

> *A good mentor is someone who has a relationship with God that has developed through the years and has a heart for sharing the lessons they have learned along the way.*
> *—Ryan, 24*

Finding a Mentor

So now you know some of the characteristics you're looking for in a mentor, but how do you find one? Here are some suggestions:

First, pray for God's wisdom. Spend time daily asking the Lord to bring to your mind and heart the right person for the right area of your life. Then open your eyes and ears and see what God does.

Second, keep your expectations realistic. Many making this transition into the real world have a perfect person in mind who will be their mentoring "savior." They are sure to be disappointed. The Messiah has already come and his name is Jesus. You're not looking for someone who's perfect. Look for a real human being who can share in your life.

Third, stay alert to potential mentors. Your mentor might be someone who lives in your neighborhood or attends your church— or he or she might be someone who doesn't have these natural connections. If the person lives far away, you might need to travel to find this person and meet only occasionally while staying in contact through email and phone calls. You never know: Your mentor might be a college professor. I had plenty of college professors who were my mentors. It was partly through their deep-rooted impact in my life that God has orchestrated the writing of this book. There are many spiritually mature Jesus-followers who could serve as your mentor. You just need to keep your eyes and ears open and you'll find them.

Keep in mind that you may want to have more than one mentor. As different seasons come and go, as you further discover the person God is helping you become, you might need a disciple who's modeling Christ in front of you: an advocate who's fighting for justice in the world or an artist who's emulating creativity. Your mentors will change over time, so your antenna should always be up. Keep looking for those who will invest in you face-to-face, but also understand that some may mentor you through books, magazine articles, sermons, or songs. Assemble a collection of mentors to help you negotiate your strategic transition into the real world.

> *A good mentor is someone who is, for the most part, spiritually sound. He or she needs to be someone you can trust and who's willing to listen to you and give you good, Christian advice.*
> —Jaclyn, 17

Becoming a Mentor

Now let me turn the tables. When you choose to customize and take control of your life the way God intended, excitement will begin to boil in your blood. The new freedom of the real world brings new freedom with your time. As you begin to pray and study Scripture more, your life will be filled to the brim. Like a dam that sprouts one little hole, then two, then eight, then forty, then BANG—it breaks wide open and you begin overflowing with love for God and others. Where does all the overflow go?

It's God's design for you to invest this extra into someone else. You need to share the overflow of your love and intimacy with God. As your faith matures, you need to mentor others.

So where can you find someone whom you might mentor? Well, look at your life. Where do you hang out? Maybe there's someone at your school or workplace. Maybe there' someone at your church or campus ministry. Keep your eyes and ears open to someone who might benefit from you humbly coming alongside of them. Don't force it. Let it happen naturally by God's divine direction.

Pray that God would show you someone in whom you might be able to invest your life. Remember that mentoring is a humble endeavor. Offering to walk alongside someone, to help that person grow in faith, is delicate work. Pray for God to orchestrate a divine appointment for you. As you're praying, begin looking for the right person to mentor. Here's a quick list of questions to ask yourself when you think you've spotted someone you might mentor:

First, is this person *teachable*? This person needs a heart willing to learn. Just as the disciples followed Jesus as students, this person will be following you (maybe with their notebook in hand), ready to learn how to better live for Jesus. Is this person's heart open to God? Do you sense any pride? These could be stumbling blocks in the mentoring relationship or teachable moments.

Second, will this person take *initiative*? Does he crave spiritual milk or solid food? This person must be willing to take the steps necessary to have a mentoring relationship with you. It can't be like pulling teeth.

Third, is this person *hungry*? The person you mentor must have a passion to grow and become all God wants her to be. Is there a spirit about her that hungers and thirsts for God?

> *My mentor is a woman who I totally respect. She's happy with whatever Jesus provides and looks to him for answers to her questions. She is in step with God. I want to follow her.*
> —Haylee, 15

Fourth, is he *faithful*? Will this person keep his commitments? Will he show up on time to your meetings and outings? Faithfulness to God is first; faithfulness to you is next. The person you mentor must be willing to commit.

Fifth, is this person *available*? This person needs to be able to devote time to the mentoring relationship. Is her schedule too full to work this in? Is she willing to drop some things that are not as important for the sake of this relationship with you? This person must make herself available for growth opportunities if this is going to work.

> *For a young girl, you should find an older woman who is strong in her faith in Jesus. Spend time with her. Listen to her wisdom: It can be so helpful for your whole life. —Gloria, 18*

Sixth, is the person you want to mentor *trustworthy*? You want to mentor someone whose character is as deep as his gifts and abilities. He doesn't have to be the "star of the show," just trustworthy. If the person is not responsible, it won't work. In addition, will this person follow through on an assignment you give him? He needs the ability to receive instructions and make things happen. Is he reliable?

Remember, you're not looking for someone who's perfect. You're just looking for someone who's eager to grow in faith. This person probably looks up to you as a model of Jesus, but are they willing to follow after you as you follow Christ?

A Model for Mentoring

There are so many mentoring relationships throughout history, starting with Scripture. Can you think of any? Here are a few: Abraham and Lot, Naomi and Ruth, Jonathan and David, Barnabas and Paul, and of course, Jesus and his disciples.[10]

10 Tim Elmore explores all these relationships in his book, *The Greatest Mentors of the Bible* (Kingdom Building Ministries, 1996). Here are some more examples to study: Jacob and Joseph; Jethro and Moses; Moses and Joshua; Deborah and

Did you realize there were so many of these relationships throughout Scripture? Look up these names, read over their stories, and think about the impact the first person in each pair had on the second.

Let's take a deeper look at one of these relationships—the relationship between two cousins, Elizabeth (the mother of John the Baptist) and Mary (the mother of Jesus). The Gospel of Luke begins with the story of Elizabeth, an older woman who had no children. One day an angel told Liz's husband Zechariah that Elizabeth would become pregnant and would give birth to a son who would become a messenger of God's good news.

But in the sixth month of that surprising pregnancy, her young cousin Mary received some even more unbelievable news from the angel Gabriel: She would become pregnant and give birth to the Messiah. No big deal, right? Wrong! This angelic meeting changed Mary's life and the course of history. This kind of news would cause the average person to go into shock and end up in the hospital. *Call 911. Mary's just fainted.*

So what does this young Jewish girl do? She immediately finds someone to tell. (You would too, wouldn't you?) She went to Liz. Apparently Mary thought highly of her. I think Mary knew she was a great lover of people. Mary got to her cousin's house and began to relay her encounter with Gabriel. I can imagine Elizabeth listening on the edge of her seat and asking questions: *What happened next? How big was Gabriel? Did he have wings? Were you scared? Tell me more! What else did he say? What did you say next?* I think there would have been great excitement in Liz's voice as Mary shared this history-shaking news.

Barak; Nehemiah and his kinsmen; Mordecai and Esther; Eli and Samuel; David and his men; David and Mephibosheth; Nathan and David; David and Solomon; Elijah and Elisha; Jehoiada and Joash; Isaiah and Hezekiah; Luke and Theophilus; Elizabeth and Mary; John the Baptizer and his disciples; Barnabas and John; Paul, Aquila, and Priscilla; Aquila, Priscilla, and Apollos; Paul and Silas; Paul and Timothy; Paul and Titus; Paul and Onesimus; Paul and Philemon; and Paul and Julius.

Liz is a great example of a mentor who invested in another's life. (You can read the whole story for yourself in Luke 1:5-56.) These two women were both available to one another and ready to listen. We all need people in our lives who will engage with us as we share big news and big events. Let your cup overflow from passion, and find someone to share your story with as you follow Jesus into college and beyond.

Questions for the Journey

1. Have you ever had a mentor or been a mentor? Describe the experience.

2. What are the benefits of having others in your life who are a little further along in their relationship with Jesus?

3. When you have questions about Jesus, the Bible, or the church, whom do you bring these questions to?

4. What steps can you take to find a mentor and be a mentor as you make this transition out of high school?

Web Resources

christianitytoday.com/history/features/heroes.html

Christian Heroes is a good place to find writings about Christian leaders throughout history.

growingleaders.com

Growing Leaders is a ministry led by Tim Elmore that is dedicated to helping young adults become all God wants them to be. It offers a variety of articles and other resources.

Book Resources

Disciple-Making Pastor, Leading Others on the Journey of Faith by Bill Hull (Baker, 2008).

Mentoring: How to Invest Your Life in Others by Tim Elmore (Wesleyan Publishing, 1995).

The Lost Art of Disciple Making by LeRoy Eims (Zondervan, 1978).

Mentoring: Confidence in Finding a Mentor and Becoming One by Bob Biehl (Broadman & Holman, 1997).

CHAPTER 13
DATING: YOUR FIT WITH A FUTURE SPOUSE

I plan to find someone who loves me for who I truly am and is a godly person. I believe God has the perfect person in store for me in my future. —Jodi, 15

Cloud Nine

I still remember the moment I spotted her in the airport. She was sitting on the terminal floor writing creative notes. Her sandy blond hair was full of curls. When she looked up at me, her beautiful bluish-green eyes (with a hint of yellow) melted my heart. I tried to talk to her but stumbled over my words. She was flying to the same place I was. Our two teams of college students had merged to cross the ocean on a short-term mission experience to Romania.

The second memory I have of her was in the middle of our time in Romania. We were on a bus heading to a ministry service location. Her black sunglasses covered her stunning eyes. I was captured by her beauty and intrigued by her mystery. Sparks were flying in my heart, but we were on a mission trip and serving Jesus. All that would have to wait until we returned home. It did.

When we returned home Laurie and I started dating. I'll admit I was caught off guard—first, by her looks, then by her heart for Jesus. The more we talked, the closer we became. Month by month, our relationship deepened. Eventually we became engaged, then married. We've been growing in our relationship with each other for 14 years and counting.

If you'd told me during our first month of dating that I'd love her more 14 years later than I did at the time, I would have said, "No way! I could never love her more than I do now. This is as good as it gets." But I would've been so wrong. My love for Laurie is miles wider and deeper today. Why? I know her so much better today than I did 14 years ago.

Do you have your own story about falling in love? Are you still hoping to meet that special someone, or are you planning to stay single? If you've dated, have your experiences been healthy or harmful?

With the right principles in place, finding the right person, dating, and marrying can be one of the most exciting journeys you'll ever take. But before we talk any more about that possibility, let's start with being single.

A Word or Two on the Single Life

Is it possible that being single is better than being married?

We all start out single. If you're reading this as you're preparing to leave high school, you're most likely single. Maybe you assume you'll find a special someone someday. Or maybe not. But let's think a little bit about the single life.

Being single is a great thing. It's not second-class status to being married, and it's not just a transitional stage. Many people in the Bible found they were able to more fully devote their lives to God as singles. The apostle Paul took full advantage of his singleness: He traveled the world, shared the Gospel of Jesus, planted churches, and found time to write most of the New Testament. Would he have been able to do that if he'd had a wife and five kids? Maybe— but he definitely took advantage of his singleness.

If you're single, celebrate your singleness. Take advantage of the benefits, because singleness is an honorable calling. Many throughout history have used their singleness to advance the kingdom—including Jesus!

There will be moments when your soul is yelling, *This is great. I have so much freedom. I'm so content.* But there might be times when you feel lonely and find yourself wishing you had another person to share your life with. In those times remember that Jesus is all you need. I know that might sound like a slogan or a bumper sticker, but it really is true. He's your closest companion, and he longs for you to draw close to him.

> *I intend to look for a woman who I can trust, who I can respect, who I can love, with whom I can imagine sharing my life. —Tom, 16*

Pursuing the Biblical Way

If you're interested in marrying one day, you might wonder if the Bible has any advice on finding your one true love. In fact, there are all kinds of different stories about how people in the Bible made the connection with that special someone. Perhaps you might want to follow these examples, but probably not:

- You might want to find an attractive prisoner of war, bring her home, shave her head, trim her nails, and give her new clothes. No kidding. This was God's idea for the Israelites back in the day (Deuteronomy 21:11-13).

- You might try marrying a prostitute to help people understand God's faithfulness. That's what Hosea did when he was told to marry Gomer (Hosea 1:1-3).

- Ladies, you might watch for a man seeking to impress you by defending your right to take well water for your flock of sheep. That's how Moses captured the heart of his wife (Exodus 2:16-21).

- Guys, you could agree to work seven years in exchange for a woman's hand in marriage. But be careful: You might get tricked into marrying the wrong woman and have to work another seven for the woman you wanted to marry. That's what happened to Jacob (Genesis 29:15-30).

- You could find a spouse by going to a party, grabbing a woman, and carrying her off to be your wife. This was the Benjamites' plan for marriage (Judges 21:9-25).

- If you prefer the gross way of winning love, try killing 200 men in battle, cutting off their foreskins, and presenting them to your future father-in-law in exchange for his daughter's hand. That's what David did (1 Samuel 18:27).

Need more ideas? How about these:

- You could become the emperor of a huge nation and hold a beauty contest. This is exactly what Xerxes did to win the heart of Esther. Well, sort of (Esther 2:3-4).

- Still desperate for a date? Maybe your parents could help. Next time you see someone you like, go home and tell your parents, "I've seen a woman I like. Now get

I want to find a man who's running as fast as he can toward God. I know that God holds my future in his hands, and that's all I need to know. —Brooke, 17

her for me." This might have been Samson's first mistake (Judges 14:1-3).

- Maybe you're being too picky. Make up for quality with quantity. Solomon had a bunch of spouses (1 Kings 11:1-3).

- If worst comes to worst, beg God to create a wife for you while you're sleeping. But be careful; it'll cost you a rib. This was Adam's story (Genesis 2:19-24).

Yes, it's true—every single one of those examples is really in the Bible. But relax: I'm not suggesting you try any of them. Times have changed a little bit. Okay, times have changed in many ways. Some of these examples had a great deal to do with the culture of the day, where a wife was often considered to be more a man's property than his partner. And it's important to remember that not all of these examples were God's idea. With marriage (as in other areas), sometimes the people of the Bible took things into their own hands, ignoring God's best for their lives.

> *A healthy dating relationship looks like a marathon, not a sprint. Both people are mature enough to know that they'll have as long as they want to get to know each other, so they don't have to do anything impure to keep the other's attention. It's a friendship. —Shae, 18*

So let's get a little more serious now. As you head out of high school, you might have had some dating experiences, or maybe not. Either way, it's critical that you lay down some relationship boundaries as you seek to become a mature, Christ-following adult.

The Goal of Dating

So what's the purpose of dating? Think about it. Why are you looking for a date? Is it to find a spouse? Is it to fulfill your sex drive? To cure your loneliness? To have a fairytale romance? Is there another reason?

From the beginning God understood that it wasn't good for Adam to be alone (Genesis 1-2). Plants and animals didn't fulfill the need for authentic friendship, companionship, and love that another human being could supply. Enter Eve, stage right! She really was Miss Right. I can imagine Adam groggily waking up from his surgery, minus a rib. He must've rubbed his eyes, yawned, laid eyes on Eve, jumped to his feet, and said, "Whoa, man!" (Wo-man....Get it? Just keep reading.)

Both men and women were made in God's image. Or, to say it another way, the image of God is fully represented by the completeness of man and woman together. Men and women are different, have you noticed? Not just physically, but in many areas and desires. They bring different qualities to relationships, but together they make up the image of God. To see the complete view of God, we must take a view of the "oneness" of woman and man. Together there is completeness, wholeness, safety, security, and love.

The difficulties for Adam and Eve start when selfishness, brokenness, and loneliness enter the world because of their choice to be like God and eat from the fruit tree in the garden. Pride caused them to realize they were naked. The true nature of the relationship was broken. If you're in a relationship and tension, miscommunication, unmet expectations, and arguments arise, blame it on Adam and Eve. Really, they started this mess. As a result, we too must take ownership of our own mistakes against God.

> *Become close friends first, then take the step to start dating. Don't put yourself in a tempting position. Share your boundaries and expectations. TAKE IT SLOW!*
> *—Stephanie, 18*

Your goal in dating should be to find the Adam to your Eve. (Or Eve to your Adam.) It's as Sid the sloth, eyes aflutter, said to Diego the saber-toothed tiger in the movie *Ice Age*: "You complete me!" We need people in our lives to make a loving connection. This love comes from friendships of all levels—but for some of us, it's found most profoundly in loving a partner for life.

True Love

Before we got married, Laurie and I decided to have some verses from the Bible engraved inside our wedding rings. The engravings read: "1 Cor. 13:4 8." It's a passage from one of Paul's letters to a church in the city of Corinth in which he talks about love. These verses are often read at weddings—but the love they describe is greater than romantic love. You can use these verses as guidelines for what it means to be loving—not only in a dating relationship with someone you might marry, but in all your relationships.

First, here are the verses:

Love is patient, love is kind. It does not envy, it does not boast, it is not proud. It does not dishonor others, it is not self-seeking, it is not easily angered, it keeps no record of wrongs. Love does not delight in evil but rejoices with the truth. It always protects, always trusts, always hopes, always perseveres. Love never fails. (1 Corinthians 13:4-8)

As you seek to become a more loving person, you may find that some words in these verses above will come naturally. Still other words will be a struggle for you. It'll become a daily choice to be patient or kind when your first impulse is to be quick-tempered or cruel. When you're hurt by someone you love, it's difficult to forget. Still, you'll need to let go of the hurt and embrace love. It's a choice we must make over and over, not only in dating and marriage but in all aspects of life. But let me go through these verses and comment on how I see them particularly reflected in dating and marriage.

More communication. Less touching. —Brooke, 17

Love is patient—even in trying circumstances. I'm very patient when things are going my way, aren't you? It's easy when things are moving along as planned. But when they aren't, that's the real test of patience. Don't be impatient. Don't rush ahead in your relationship. I know, "He's soooooo good-looking," and, "She's hot." Use your brain more than your heart. It'll save you hurt and bring health later to your relationship.

Love is kind when faced with unkindness. It's so easy to hurt one another and so easy to forget to do those little kind deeds. Love chooses to be kind regardless of the response because love is committed to giving, not receiving. The person you love might be difficult at times, but love chooses to serve no matter what.

Love is never jealous or vain. You shouldn't worry about whom he's with when he's not with you. If you have jealously issues, you're not expressing love. Talk about it. Clear it up. Love isn't jealous.

Love gives when it feels more natural to be selfish and hold on. It's a challenge you'll face throughout your life. Suppose you've finally finished your physics paper and you're ready to relax. You look over and see that your loved one is still struggling with their paper. Do you offer to help or pretend you didn't notice? Love gets up and keeps going. Love gives a little more.

Love keeps no record of wrongs. Love chooses to forgive and forget. Has someone you love wronged you? Chances are good that you've been hurt already. Don't let this slow you down from trusting and loving one another. Do all you can to move into the future with freedom.

Love takes joy in being fully truthful because the truth sets you free. Don't hide anything from the one you love. Share it tactfully, carefully, and in the right timing. Always live in truth and you will find peace.

Love believes, trusts, hopes, and keeps on keeping on. If no one else believes in you, make sure you believe in the one you love. Love never fails.

You can be sure there will be stretching times when your faith in God and your love will be tested. You'll be at your limit sometimes and wonder how you can keep going. You can! Love will keep you going. Love from God is your anchor in the storm. In those stretching times, may you find yourselves holding hands in love, and may you find this to be enough.

The Physical Side

It's natural for two people in love to feel physically attracted to each other. But our physical drive can too easily fall into the trap of becoming a desire for quick, selfish gratification and pleasure. The flipside of love is selfishness, and lust is driven by selfishness. Test your actions against 1 Corinthians 13. If you're putting the other's needs before your own, you're most likely pursuing in a truly loving manner. But if you're just in the relationship to get something for yourself, you can be sure it's not love. Test your motives in the relationship. Are you dying to self or just dying for a date?

As people pursue love, they often face a question regarding their physical relationship: "How far is too far?" Some people will say: "Well, as long as we don't have *sexual intercourse*, we're okay—right?" I think these questions really have to do with the relationship between commitment and sexual activity.

The longer a couple is together, the more commitment typically exists in the relationship. This isn't always the case, but most of the time if a couple has been together for a long amount of time, there's a higher commitment level. Sometimes couples are together way too long. They know the relationship isn't headed toward a life-long commitment in marriage, but they refuse to cut if off for whatever reason (possibly because they're way too far along emotionally and physically). Other times they're just "friends with benefits," taking advantage of each other physically. They think they can handle it, but they're

> I want to find a woman who I care for deeply and get to know for as long as it takes until I'm sure I want to spend the rest of my life with her. I'll stay content, telling myself it's worth the wait. —Bradley, 16

actually emotionally and spiritually hurting themselves and their partner.

In a healthy relationship the level of physical activity won't exceed the level of commitment. Healthy relationships move along slowly and deliberately. Take a look at the chart below:

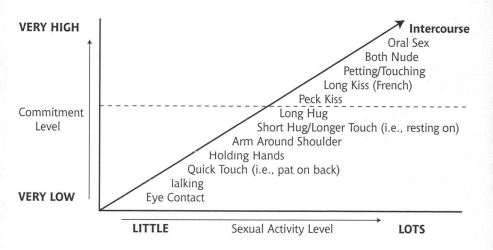

In my estimation the biggest obstacle to obtaining a healthy, loving dating relationship with another person is the tension between the horizontal and vertical lines. The problem occurs when the *commitment* and amount of time the couple has spent together is low, but the level of *sexual activity* is high.

The next question many dating couples ask? "But how much time needs to pass before we can (fill in the blank)?" Here's my suggestion: Don't worry about moving up the arrow to the right. It will happen on it's own as time passes, conversations are had, the commitment level grows, and trust is built. This can take months, even years to build; that's a good thing. Take a look at the dotted line. When you pass the dotted line, it's easy to reach a point of no return where your will power isn't strong enough to resist sexual temptation. That's why certain levels of sexual activity belong only within the life-long commitment of a marriage. I'd suggest you avoid going beyond the dotted line until you have entered marriage with a life-long partner. Remember 1 Corinthians 13? The key is to stay focused on your own relationship with Jesus and allow God to direct you as a couple.

Suppose Jimmy and Pam hook up at a party and have sexual intercourse. They spent two hours together and have no real commitment to each other, but they engaged in acts God wants us to save for marriage. Sexual intercourse, as well as many of the physical acts leading to sexual intercourse, is reserved for marriage only. The emotional, spiritual, and sometimes physical damage that can occur from engaging in these activities outside the commitment of marriage is devastating. And you know what's tragic? Night after night, more and more lives are devastated by sexual sin.

I think most of us intuitively understand this. Of a survey of 3,000 women, 80 percent said they regretted having casual sex before marriage.[11] We know before it happens that it's not God's best for us; it's not healthy. This kind of living damages future relationships and slows down your hope of finding Mr. or Mrs. Right. Every time you decide to engage in temporary pleasure with someone you're not married to, you damage yourself and the health of your future relationships.

Here's another scenario: Ed and Sally have dated for four months, during the course of which the physical side of their relationship has moved from holding hands and hugging to kissing and petting—and last night they had sexual intercourse for the first time. Their self-control weakened throughout the months until it disappeared altogether. Their desire for one another (lust) became a driving force in their relationship. Love for God, and love for one another, is no longer driving their relationship.

---

11 Statistics were taken from *A Girl's Guide to Casual Sex* (Ten Speed Press, 2004).

Ed and Sally are both followers of Jesus but struggling spiritually in their relationships with God and each other. They think they're in love, but according to God's best for their lives, their actions are selfish. They finally break off the relationship, and it's emotionally damaging to both. Each day, this scenario happens over and over in the real world.

What If I've Already Crossed the Line?

If your physical relationship with someone has already gone further than it should have, seek God. Ask him to forgive you. Ask the person you had relations with to forgive you. Admit your selfishness.

Here is the good news: Regardless of what has happened in the past—whether it was last night or last year—God longs to have a close relationship with you. He wants your heart right now, whether you're returning to him again or coming to him for the very first time. No matter what your mistakes have been, there's nothing so bad that he won't forgive you (Mark 3:28).

You can always have a fresh start at building a healthy, God-honoring relationship. Jesus won't hold your mistakes against you in the future, but he does want you to change your way of thinking so you won't continue to make the same mistakes as you grow into a mature, Jesus-following adult. Be encouraged: His mercies are new every morning (Psalm 25:6).

After asking God for forgiveness, set boundaries—today! Look at the chart and ask yourself how far you'll move in future relationships as you seek to truly love your dating partner.

Keeping Love Alive

As you enter a relationship and pursue love with someone else, commit yourself to serving that person. Look for ways to fan the flames of love. Go on a picnic, take a walk together, watch a movie with a group, find something to laugh about, or write each other encouraging notes. As you head through the steps of dating to engagement and marriage, never let romance wane. It takes effort to be romantic, but it's worth it. Romance isn't just about sexual attraction; it involves the whole being of a person. Having a great conversation can be romantic.

When you're angry, deal with it. Do your best to get rid of anger before the day is over. Never talk *at* one another; this isn't loving. Never speak loudly at one another unless the house (or apartment or dorm room or Starbucks) is on fire. Don't try to find fault with one another; give the benefit of the doubt. If there's a disagreement remember the goal isn't to win the argument but to love one another in the process.

Never leave one another without a warm word (and a loving embrace, if you've been dating a while). As you build trust with this person, begin to save the very best events of your day for the one you love; it's always the most fun the first time you share it. Always keep Jesus first in your individual lives and you'll be amazed at how your dating and marriage relationship flourishes.

Most of all, keep God at the center of your relationship. Maybe you've seen the following triangle diagram. God is at the top; you and the person who "caught your eye" are on opposite sides of the base.

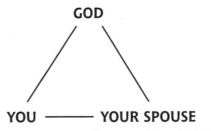

GOD

YOU ——— YOUR SPOUSE

As each of you seeks to grow closer to God you'll grow closer to one another. The more intimate you are in your relationship with the one who is Love, the more in love you'll become with each another. Get closer to God through studying the Bible and talking to him all the time. When two people in love each pursue God individually, it's amazing how unstoppable they become together for bringing the kingdom of God to earth. I've known many couples who individually loved Jesus and together were amazing in their impact on the world. This kind of relationship isn't always easy, but it is loving.

As you head from high school to life after high school, make peace with the past and move into the future, striving to work primarily on your personal relationship with Jesus. If God brings a special someone into your life, take it slow, lovingly moving forward in the relationship. Keep in mind that healthy dating leads to a healthy marriage, and the marriage is more important than the wedding.

Questions for the Journey

1. What does healthy dating look like?

2. From this day forward, how can you make sure you don't cross any lines in your relationships with others?

3. Do you see your body as something holy or sacred? What difference does it make to see your body as sacred versus something to be used and destroyed?

4. What qualities do you think are most important in a Christian marriage?

Web Resources

sexetc.org

This is a Web site by teens for teens where students can discuss topics of sex, parenting, body image, alcohol and drugs, and many other issues. It's a great place to find out what teens think about such matters.

christianitytoday.com/search/?query=dating&x=0&y=0
Here are several articles on dating from a Christian perspective at *Christianity Today.*

Book Resources

Boundaries in Dating by Henry Cloud and John Townsend (Zondervan, 2001).

Questions You Can't Ask Your Mama About Sex by Craig Gross and Mike Foster (Zondervan, 2005).

Sacred Marriage by Gary Thomas (Zondervan, 2002).

Single Adult Passages by Carolyn Koons and Michael Anthony (Baker, 1995).

CHAPTER 14
GOD'S FAMILY: YOUR FIT WITH THE CHURCH

A community of believers reminds us we're not alone on this journey. As different and diverse as we may be, we all have something in common that unites us. We can all encourage and support one another as we grow closer to Jesus. —Ryan, 24

Homesick

The invitation came from a classmate in elementary school. "Jeff, would you like to sleep over at my house?" I was speechless. No one had asked me that before! I didn't want to hurt Tim's feelings, so I said, "Yes, but I have to ask my parents."

Twenty-four hours later, the deal was sealed. That Friday after school I was heading over to Tim's house to spend the night.

I'd never been to Tim's house before. The minute I arrived that Friday

> *The body of believers keeps me accountable in my walk with God and encourages me if I'm down.*
> *—Stephanie, 18*

I started comparing his house with mine. It smelled different. It looked different. His parents were different. The furniture was different. The food was different. The TV shows were different. His bedroom was different. It all felt very uncomfortable and, well, very different. And like a lot of first-time sleepover participants, I soon felt very homesick. I'm not embarrassed to admit I wanted my mommy. As soon as that "different meal" at that "different kitchen table" was over, I called my parents. They came and picked me up and took me to the comfort, safety, and familiarity of my own home.

Have you ever been homesick? I think we all know how hard it can be to feel far from home. We want to be in a place where we're known and where we belong.

I think church is exactly that kind of home, that place of safety and belonging. The church isn't a building; it's a group of people. The church is made up of people who long to know and love Jesus with all of their lives. It's a group of people serving one another and the world around them. Throughout history, from the first church to the many expressions of the local church today, God has longed (and still longs) for us to be in community with other believers. Church is our place to belong.

In the book of Acts, we're given a quick outline of what the first church was up to. Luke, the book's author, tells us the believers "devoted themselves to the apostles' teaching and to fellowship, to the breaking of bread and to prayer" (Acts 2:42). In an age of megachurches with entertainment programs and big budgets, it's possible to lose sight of the purpose of the local church.

Church helps me know I'm not alone. It's not easy when everyone else doesn't believe in what you do; it's kind of frustrating. Having other people makes it less stressful. When I'm struggling, they usually have pretty good advice. —Candice, 17

As you make your way into adulthood, you need to settle into a local body of believers. You might've heard it said that church membership is optional. This might sound nice, but it's just not what God thinks according to his Word.

Houston, We Have a Problem

A recent study by the Southern Baptist organization LifeWay Research found that 70 percent of 18-year-olds who attend church regularly in high school quit by age 23. The majority of those young adults eventually return to a local church, but often not until they're married and sometimes not until they have children. More than a third of the people who've left the local church (34 percent) still haven't returned by age 30.[12] Some never return. This is a tragedy.

> A community of Jesus-followers helps me by keeping me on the right path with God. They help me reach my goals in life without as many distractions along the way. —Jodi, 15

The good news? Many young people are connecting with vibrant campus ministries and spending time in community with other believers their age. This is important if you're heading off to college. I love campus ministries—I was on Fellowship of Christian Athletes leadership all four of my undergraduate years. Campus ministries are very important. Please get connected.

But even if you find and get involved with a great campus ministry, it's still important to get connected with a local church. There are many passages of Scripture that instruct all believers to deeply connect to a local faith community. Interestingly, Scripture refers to the church as the body of Christ. This metaphor is powerful. Without you, the church is missing some parts. Really. The body must have all of its parts to function in proper order. Just as the body can't function properly without an eye, ear, or big toe (you need it for balance), every local community of faith in Jesus needs a complete body to be healthy.

---

12 These statistics, which appeared on the Christianity Today Web site, were drawn from the August 6, 2007, issue of USA Today. Accessed May 23, 2008, at http://www.christianitytoday.com/le/2007/004/10.15.html.

Paul talked about all of this in his letter to a church in the city Corinth (1 Corinthians 12:12-31). Paul uses a powerful metaphor of the body to communicate how important it is for you to be connected. You have a part to play in the local church. You might be a hand, foot, ear, or nerve. These are used to accomplish God's purposes on Earth, to advance the kingdom. No member is more important than another. Just because one guy stands in front of all those people and teaches doesn't make him more important than the guy who works behind the scenes in the kitchen. We're all vital and we all need to work together. Within the local church, you'll discover the fullness of whom Christ made you to be, who you are, and where you belong.

> *The church is your support group, your true friends. They'll stand with you no matter what help bring you back if you ever fall away. They're your anchor, your life raft, your survival kit; you can't make it through the hostile waters of life without them. They're invaluable. —Shae, 18*

Paul also says that when one member of the body hurts, the whole body is hurt. If you stub your toe, it's hard not to think about your hurting toe. Your whole body hurts. In another way, when one person falls short of using their gifts, abilities, and passions to their fullest potential, everyone suffers. The church needs everyone to be serving in the right spot for the fullest impact.

The Hope of the World

Bill Hybels, senior pastor at Willow Creek Community Church in Chicago, Illinois, says the church is the "hope of the world." I think he's right. Yes, Jesus is the ultimate hope of the world, but if we don't unite with Christ as the head of the church, if we don't all come together as believers of Jesus, we won't be living up to all God has for us.

The church should make a difference in its local community and the world. If a church doesn't reach out and touch the needs of those who surround it, it really isn't being a church. If a local body of believers suddenly got up and left, the surrounding community should feel the loss because this was the group who was caring for the elderly, the hurting, the suffering, the homeless, and the outcast. The body of believers is so important to God's kingdom plan that Jesus declared the gates of hell wouldn't prevail against it (Matthew 16:13-19).

Local churches come in all shapes and sizes. You might prefer pews or folding chairs. Perhaps you like classic hymns, or maybe you'd rather hear the songs you listen to on Christian radio. Maybe you prefer a church where the preacher speaks for only 15 minutes (good luck!), or one where the worship includes visual arts. You might prefer a church that meets on the beach over one with candles and stained-glass windows. No matter what your personal preferences are, find a local church you can commit to. Even if you know you'll only be there for a few years, plug in, connect with people, become a member, take the senior pastor out to lunch, serve in your areas of giftedness, and make a huge kingdom difference. Become part of a community of believers who are serving God with faithfulness—teaching the Scriptures, breaking bread together (including the Lord's Supper), baptizing new believers, praying with and for one another, fellowshipping with joy, being authentic in their relationships, and serving the world for the sake of advancing the kingdom of God (Acts 2:42-44).

Jesus is passionate about the church. All four Gospels tell the story of Jesus overturning the tables in his Father's house because of the hiked temple costs and hypocritical living. The disciples sat back and watched, probably wondering if Jesus had lost his mind, until they remembered how the psalmist said, "Zeal for your house will consume me" (Psalm 69:9; John 2:17).

> Community brings encouragement, mostly. Additionally, I believe the prayer of many is more powerful than the prayer of one.
> —John, 16

As a Jew, Jesus understood the temple as the house of God. Today, those who seek to follow Jesus are the collective temple of God and comprise the church (1 Corinthians 6:19). Jesus has chosen to live not only everywhere, all the time, but he's also chosen to live inside each of his followers (Colossians 1:27). Today the house of God is the body of Christ, taking the great news of Jesus to a desperate world. If you aren't connected with a local body of believers right now, pay attention to that homesickness you're feeling. The local church needs you and you need the local church.

The writer of Hebrews offer us a great final word about the mission of the church: "Let us consider how we might spur one another on toward love and good deeds, not giving up meeting together, as some are in the habit of doing, but encouraging one another—and all the more as you see the Day approaching" (Hebrews 10:24-25).

Questions for the Journey

1. Would you rather follow Jesus with people around you or do it alone?

2. What troubles you about the local church? What gives you the most joy about the local church?

3. How do you see yourself being connected to the body of Christ using your gifts and abilities?

4. How will you be proactive to get connected to a local church when you leave high school?

Web Resources

youthwalk.org

> Youth Walk (from Walk Thru the Bible Ministries) is an online devotional magazine for students to help them navigate the Bible, get to know God through it, and answer his call to live the adventure of following Christ.

christianitytoday.com/search/index.html?query=finding+a+church&category=0

> Here are several articles about finding a local church home.

godweb.org/findachurch.htm

> This site provides great tips on how to find a local church home.

Book Resources

Finding a Church You Can Love and Loving the Church You've Found by Kevin G. Harney and Sherry Harney (Zondervan, 2003).

The Church in Transition by Tim Conder (Zondervan, 2006).

They Like Jesus but Not the Church by Dan Kimball (Zondervan, 2008).

The Church Unleashed by Frank Tillapaugh (Regal, 1982).

Death of the Church by Mike Regele (Zondervan, 1995).

CONCLUSION
THE NEXT 22 ¾ DAYS OF FOLLOWING JESUS

I'm extremely excited to get out into the real world and become who God intends for me to be, but I know I need to learn how to keep my priorities in line and use self-discipline before I'll be completely ready for it. —Jaclyn, 17

Take It Slow

You've reached the final chapter of the book. If you've read every word so far, I congratulate you. Well done! If you're picking up this book for the first time and you figured you'd skip to the last chapter and see how the story ends—well, that's okay, but you may want to go back and start at the beginning. If you're the kind of reader who jumps around in a book, or if you've been keeping this book on a shelf for a rainy day, that's fine, too. Whatever your reading style, I hope you're finding this book an encouragement in your walk with Jesus.

As I think about you heading out the door to serve Jesus, I remember a morning when my daughter was leaving to catch the school bus after a wintry ice storm. She was hurrying down the driveway with her head raised high, taking long, confident strides as if it were a beautiful, sunny summer day. I knew if she continued down the icy sidewalk at that quick pace, or if she started to run to catch the bus, she'd fall, get hurt, and maybe cry. (And miss the bus!) So as any good parent would do, I yelled:

"Lillian, slow down and take shorter steps. Watch out for ice!"

"Okay," came the reply.

That's my simple advice to you as you make this exciting transition from the world of high school to the world of college and beyond. This transition will require firm footing and good timing. There are many pitfalls and slippery slopes to watch out for in a world filled with temptations and ungodly pleasures. If you run into this life too quickly without looking both ways, you'll slip and fall—and the pain will be more than that of a bruise. So take it slow, enjoy the journey, and keep your eyes fixed on Jesus, the One who's the same, yesterday, today, and forever (Hebrews 13:8).

From Child to Adult

The goal of this book has been to help you move toward becoming a mature, Jesus-following adult. It's been about creating space for you to transition from being a child, who's largely dependent on your parents, to a young adult, who takes increasing responsibility for your own direction while understanding that we're all dependent on God.

Throughout this book I've attempted to give you practical advice for your journey of faith. As you move from childlike faith to mature, adult faith, here are some additional areas to think about.

Take a look at each line on the chart below and ask yourself, "Is my faith more childlike or mature in this area?"[13]

Childlike Faith	Mature Adult Faith
Good Christians don't have pain and disappointment.	God uses our pain and disappointments to make us more faithful followers of Christ.
God helps those who help themselves.	God helps those who admit their own helplessness.
God wants to make us happy.	God wants to make us holy; more like Christ in our words and actions.
Faith will always help us explain what God is doing because things always work my way.	Faith helps us stand under God's divine control even when we have no idea what God's doing.
The closer we get to God, the more perfect we become.	The closer we get to God, the more we become aware of our own sinfulness and dependence on someone to save us.
Mature Christians have all the answers.	Mature Christians can honestly wrestle with tough questions because we trust God has the answers.
Good Christians are always strong.	Our strength is admitting our weakness and dependence on God.
We go to a local church because our friends are there, we have great leaders, and we get something out of it.	We go to church because we belong to the body of Christ and long to serve.

13 This chart was adapted from Mark Devries' *Family-Based Youth Ministry* (InterVarsity, 1994).

So where do you find yourself on this chart? Which set of statements best match your own beliefs? Wherever you find yourself, keep in mind that faith is a journey; becoming mature in your faith doesn't happen overnight. I hope you'll keep reading and praying through the themes and chapters of this book so you can continue to become the mature, Jesus-following adult God intends you to be.

Your Next 22 ¾ Days in the Real World

I've heard it said that it takes 22 days to develop a new habit or break an old one. This means that you have to do something at least 22 days in a row before it begins to become part of your everyday routine. So given all we've talked about in this book, the next 22 ¾ days or so (if you're like me, you might need that extra ¾ of a day) are critical. Whether you're just out of high school or have been out for a while, immediately begin to develop God-honoring habits and break the ones that aren't.

Take another look at the three big themes of this book: *Identity*, *Choices*, and *Belonging*. Below are the questions connected to each theme that I attempted to answer throughout the chapters of this book. Can you answer these questions for yourself with conviction?

ONE – *Identity*: Who am I? Who am I suppose to be and what do I know to be true? Can I doubt sometimes?

TWO – *Choices*: Do my decisions really matter? How much control of my life do I have? How do I handle the new responsibilities coming my way as an adult? How will I handle college? Is it okay if I'm stressed out?

THREE – *Belonging*: Where do I fit? What does this world have for me? What does God have for me? Where do family, friends, and dating fit? How important is it for me to connect to the local church?

Go back and review the topics addressed in each chapter under these themes. Think about what you can do to develop positive habits in each of these areas. Here are some steps to help you in the process:

First, decide exactly what you want to do. In what area do you need to develop a new habit or change an old one? Maybe you want to nail down your *Identity* and form holy habits, like Scripture study. You might decide to read a Psalm, a section from Proverbs, or a chapter from the gospel of Mark each day for the next several weeks. Maybe you need to prioritize your relationships or improve your study habits. Decide what habits you can develop to help you grow in the areas where you need to focus. Then write those ideas down and post them where you'll see them every day, like your bathroom mirror, book bag, car, or in the shower. (If you choose the shower, don't forget to put them inside a Ziploc bag first!) Be as specific as possible; specific actions lead to specific habits.

Second, make time for what you want to do. Again, it takes around 22 days to form a habit, so schedule at least 22 days on your calendar and don't let anything get in the way. Schedule time with God. Schedule time for relationships. Schedule opportunities to have fun. Schedule, schedule, schedule. As you head into the real world, your time management will be completely dependent upon your keeping a good schedule. If you miss one of your scheduled days, don't stress out. Give yourself grace, but do your best to be consistent and dedicated to what you've decided to do so it can become a positive, God-honoring habit.

Third, as you notice the action becoming a habit, congratulate yourself. But don't stop there. Keep going with the habit, but add another action for the next 22, then another and so on, until you're doing those things you want to do as part of your daily routine without even thinking about them...like brushing your teeth, riding a bike, sleeping.... (Okay, maybe some of you need to develop this habit.)

Finally, remember the goal: following Jesus. That's the point of these habits and the point of this book. My heart's desire has been to help you grow into mature Jesus-followers for the long haul. If you apply the principles of this book, you'll be well on your way.

Traps to Avoid for the Next 22 ¾ Days and Beyond

Take a deep breath—we're almost done. But before you close this book, I want to give you my list of the most common mistakes made by those who are leaving high school and entering the real world. These top-10 traps are in no particular order, but they all represent very real temptations for you to avoid as you head into this next chapter of your life. Stay alert and keep clear of these traps. Drum roll, please:

1. Listen more than you talk. Many leaving the high school world think they have it all figured out. Hopefully you've realized you don't have all the answers. Be careful to express your opinions and "expert advice" at the right times in the right places. If you don't, you could find yourself in trouble with friends, co-workers, professors, church leaders, and others around you. Remember to listen more than you talk; this is proven to produce wisdom.

2. Exercise. Many of those entering the real world forget to exercise. Some of you might have been active in high school, but many of you were not all-star athletes. Start a habit of exercising immediately.

3. Draw healthy boundaries. Many leaving high school drop their moral boundaries and become sexually active. Don't put yourself in this position (literally)! Live for love, not lust. Set your boundaries now so you don't find yourself naked in the bed of someone you barely know. The consequences could send your life on a major detour for the worse. You don't want to go there.

4. Have fun. Many leaving high school forget to have real, healthy fun. College is about getting an education, preparing to join the workforce, and bringing home some cash, but these years are also about growing into a mature Jesus-follower for the rest of your life. This is a fun time, and God invented fun. So make sure you laugh and enjoy the abundant life he created for you to have in college and beyond.

5. Stay away from drugs. You'd think that being a follower of Jesus would dissuade someone from using drugs. But like sex, temptations will come at you in the real world like a pack of wild wolves pursuing a deer. Be on guard! Don't go down this path—you may think you can experiment with this stuff safely, but you can easily become addicted and lose your relationships, job, and health. Drugs will destroy your life.

6. Eat healthy. Many leaving high school eat everything in arms' reach. With the opportunity to make all their own choices about food, they think they've died and gone to heaven. All-you-can-eat everything...every meal! It's great—great until the second semester is over and they realize the reality of the "freshman 15." On the flipside, some students don't eat enough (or at all) and endanger their own health. Be wise in your eating habits: Your identity in Jesus is positively or negatively affected by them.

7. Don't abuse your freedom. Many who've recently been released from parental boundaries decide to party it up. They drink too much, do things they don't remember the next morning, and start down the path of destruction. Decide now that you won't put yourself in situations that can negatively affect your studies, class attendance, church participation, friendships, and overall health. You don't want this kind of reputation, especially as a Jesus-follower.

8. Avoid procrastination. Many leaving high school wait till the last minute to get things done. Consequently they fall behind. Maybe you could get away with that kind of approach in high school, but it's time to wake up. In college and in the workforce,

waiting till the last minute will get you failed or fired. Walking out of high school into the real world can be like stepping on a treadmill that's already moving 100 miles per hour. Be careful—you could get hurt. Once you're in the groove of college or the workforce, stay on pace so you don't get behind.

9. Stay involved. Many college-aged individuals sit in their dorm room or apartment when they're not in class or at work. It's hard to imagine, but some choose not to get involved in extracurricular activities. In college, there are plenty of extracurricular things to do. There are many campus ministries and local churches to plug in to. The options are endless, so take advantage of your interests and stay active...but balance them with studying and other activities.

10. Take Jesus with you. This one is the key. Many leaving high school forget to take Jesus along. By this point in the book, I hope you understand the importance of making a relationship with the real Jesus a central part of your life. He loves you passionately and only wants the best for you. Follow him and let him guide your identity, choices, and belonging.

The Final Word

Not long ago, I was sitting at an airport gate in Chicago waiting for my next flight. I was minding my own business when I clearly heard the following words: "Blessed be the name of the Lord...Blessed be his naaaammmmeee!" I looked up and saw a young guy bobbing his head to the music on his iPod, completely clueless of the volume level. The thirty-something guy next to him turned and looked at the kid with an angry scowl on his face. But I noticed another guy standing between the rocking teenager and I. He had white hair and looked to be at least 60 years old. Our eyes met. He knew I'd heard the music and was looking at me with a smile, shaking his head in approval as if to say, "That's a great tune! Blessed be his name!"

So here's my invitation to you as you begin this new season of life: As you leave high school, take that tune with you. Take Jesus with you for the long haul. God really is good. Think about the blessings he's given you: You can read, think, breathe, and eat. *You're alive.* God loves you regardless of what you've done and what challenges you face. Blessed be his name. As you grow older, don't become like the grumpy thirty-something in the airport. Instead, take the music with you and crank it up. Keep bobbing your head to that beat till you're old and gray.

Well, this is the end of the book but the beginning of the rest of your life. May God unleash you into this world as an unstoppable force. May you bring his kingdom to Earth as you follow Jesus into college and beyond.

APPENDIX
A NOTE TO PASTORS, PARENTS, AND YOUTH PROFESSIONALS

Now to him who is able to do immeasurably more than all we ask or imagine, according to his power that is at work within us, to him be glory in the church and in Christ Jesus throughout all generations, for ever and ever! Amen. (Ephesians 3:20-21)

I hope you've found this book a useful tool in helping the students in your congregation or care as they transition into the real world after high school. Let me share a few additional thoughts that will sharpen your discipleship skills.

The Gap Is Getting Wider

Times are changing fast! By the time you read this, the latest trends in music, language, and fashion among youth will have changed several times since I wrote these words. And students themselves are changing more rapidly than ever before. The dynamics of the transition from high school to college and beyond are different than when you and I were that age.

You may already realize the period of adolescence (Latin meaning *to grow up*) is much longer than it once was. For today's students, the time of transition begins earlier and ends later. The best way to measure the start of these years is with the onset of puberty (Latin meaning *adult*), and these physical changes are now occurring earlier than ever before. Yet the end of this period of transition, which usually coincides with a student's leaving home, is now happening later, sometimes not until the early 20s. It's critical that we help students bring a biblical perspective to issues of identity, choices, and belonging as they negotiate these years. Take a look at the line diagrams below; they illustrate the widening gap of adolescence.[14]

Pre-1900

Childhood   *Adulthood*

Years: 0   14   16

Before 1900, kids moved from childhood to adulthood almost overnight. There is very little gray area above representing adolescence. Before the Industrial Revolution (which gave birth to factory employment) children worked on the farm with the family and stayed on the farm when they became adults. As soon as childhood ended with the onset of puberty, marriage and childbearing followed. This is the *Little House on the Prairie* life. Fast forward to 1980...

---

14 There are many resources for these findings, including *Disconnected* by Chap and Dee Clark, pages 60-69.

1980

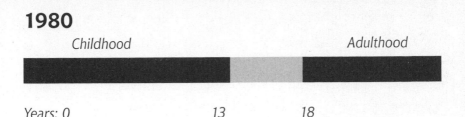

Childhood

Adulthood

Years: 0   13   18

By 1980, we see the gray period representing adolescence has expanded from the onset of puberty at about age 13 to the end of the high-school years at age 18. It was around this time that most church and parachurch ministries decided to follow the lead of the public school system and separate junior high and senior high ministries. Now let's take a look at the current situation...

Today

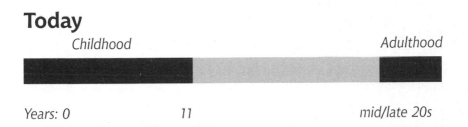

Childhood

Adulthood

Years: 0   11   mid/late 20s

Today, the gray gap in the diagram above has widened further. The average age for the onset of puberty is about 11. The full transition to adulthood often extends to the mid-to-late 20s. It's no wonder we're seeing college and young-adult ministries growing within many churches in the same way youth ministries did a few decades ago. Young adults are a new demographic group that demands new outreach strategies.

With the increase in the length of adolescence, it's no wonder students are having a more difficult time maintaining their relationship with Jesus after they leave high school. Who knows when the gap will stop widening? (For more insights about the nature of these changes, see the books listed at the end of this Appendix.)

Using the Book in Your Ministry

The adolescents you're working with in ministry, whether they're living at home or have recently left, are still searching for answers to many questions surrounding the three critical themes of this book: *Identity, Choices,* and *Belonging.* I believe this book can be used strategically in your church, ministry, and family. Here are some tactics for using *Following Jesus into College and Beyond* with young people in your high school, college, and young adult ministries.

You might want to consider planning your curriculum around the themes of this book. The areas of *Identity, Choices,* and *Belonging* can provide purpose and direction for biblical teaching, special programs, small groups, mentoring relationships, retreats, and mission trips. Let the book prompt your creativity in addressing the big questions adolescents are asking (in their hearts, if not aloud) during these critical years. As I've noted in each chapter, the Bible has wisdom to address these critical questions of adolescent development. Ask yourself: "How can I use these themes and topics to help my young people follow Jesus more faithfully?"

You can use the discussion questions at the end of each chapter as a starting point for your interactions with students who are graduating high school and entering college and beyond. As pastors, parents, and other youth professionals, we're responsible for helping them negotiate these topics. The resources referenced at the end of each chapter may prompt your own further research and study. The questions provided can be used in one-on-one mentoring times, with small groups, and in larger group environments. You may want to buy a copy of the book for each student in your ministry and have the group members work through it together.

I'm sure I don't need to tell you how critical it is to help high school and college students understand what the world will throw at them. We have the responsibility and privilege of discipling the next generation until they're ready to follow Jesus for the long haul! Your loving investment and partnership won't go unnoticed by our heavenly Father. If I can help you further by consulting or training your ministry leaders, or by speaking in your ministry, please don't hesitate to contact me through Zondervan (www.Zondervan.com) or my blog (www.sacredoutfitter.blogspot.com).

Blessings as you help your students follow Jesus into college and beyond!

Even when I am old and gray, do not forsake me, my God, till I declare your power to the next generation, your mighty acts to all who are to come.
(Psalm 71:18)

Further Reading on Understanding and Ministering to Adolescents

Adolescence and Emerging Adulthood by Jeffrey Arnett (Prentice Hall, 2006).

Hurt: Inside the World of Today's Teenagers by Dr. Chap Clark (Baker Academic, 2004).

Disconnected: Parenting Teens in a MySpace World by Dr. Chap Clark (Baker Books, 2008).

Family-Based Youth Ministry by Mark DeVries (InterVarsity, 1994).

All Grown Up and No Place to Go by David Elkind (Perseus Books Group,1998).

Family Ministry by Diana Garland (InterVarsity, 1999).

Youth Culture 101 by Walt Mueller (Zondervan, 2007).

You are here for a reason. God is calling you to change the world. How will you do that? Inside the pages of this book, you'll discover that God has definitely created you for a purpose, and you'll learn what that purpose is. So, dive in, explore who you are and what you're made to do—so you can change the whole world.

Leave a Footprint—Change the Whole World
Tim Baker
RETAIL $9.99
ISBN 978-0-310-27885-6

Our planet is no longer the paradise God created. In this book you'll learn how to honor God in the choices you make, and you'll begin to understand the impact those choices have on the environment. Sixteen-year-old Emma Sleeth will help you see how you can make a difference at school, around the house, and all over the world.

It's Easy Being Green
One Student's Guide to Serving God and Saving the Planet
Emma Sleeth
RETAIL $12.99
ISBN 978-0-310-27925-9

Visit www.planetwisdom.com or your local bookstore.

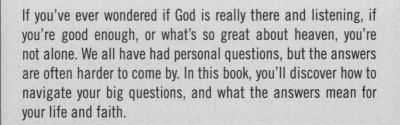

If you've ever wondered if God is really there and listening, if you're good enough, or what's so great about heaven, you're not alone. We all have had personal questions, but the answers are often harder to come by. In this book, you'll discover how to navigate your big questions, and what the answers mean for your life and faith.

Living with Questions
Dale Fincher
RETAIL $9.99
ISBN 978-0-310-27664-0

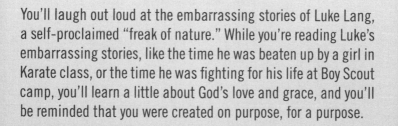

You'll laugh out loud at the embarrassing stories of Luke Lang, a self-proclaimed "freak of nature." While you're reading Luke's embarrassing stories, like the time he was beaten up by a girl in Karate class, or the time he was fighting for his life at Boy Scout camp, you'll learn a little about God's love and grace, and you'll be reminded that you were created on purpose, for a purpose.

I AM Standing Up
True Confessions of a Total Freak of Nature
Luke Lang
RETAIL $9.99
ISBN 978-0-310-28325-6

Visit www.planetwisdom.com or your local bookstore.

Love This! contains real-life stories of people like you who've found ways to love their neighbors. It will challenge you to make a difference in your world by loving people who are often ignored or unloved—the homeless, the addicted, the elderly, those of different races, even your enemies—and show you tangible ways you can demonstrate that love.

Love This!
Learning to Make It a Way of Life, Not Just a Word
Andy Braner
RETAIL $12.99
ISBN 978-0-310-27380-3

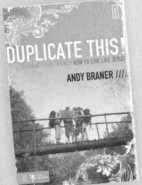

Before Jesus left his disciples he said to them, "Go and make disciples of all nations." It was a command for everyone who follows Jesus. But what does it mean?

In *Duplicate This!* you'll learn the foundations of discipleship, and what it means to make a disciple, and you'll be equipped to walk with your friends as they learn what it looks like to follow Jesus.

Duplicate This!
Showing Your Friends How to Live Like Jesus
Andy Braner
RETAIL $12.99
ISBN 978-0-310-27754-5

Visit www.planetwisdom.com or your local bookstore.

If you don't understand why you feel, act, or think the way you do now, and life used to be so simple, you're not alone—you're growing up! Listen to other girls like you, and two women who know a lot about what you're going through. You'll start to understand who you are, and you'll see the wonderful person you're becoming.

Growing Up without Getting Lost
Discovering Your Identity in Christ
Melissa Trevathan & Sissy Goff
RETAIL $16.99
ISBN 978-0-310-27917-4

Visit www.planetwisdom.com or your local bookstore.

Brooklyn Lindsey grew up dreaming of being a supermodel. But it wasn't until she became a youth pastor that she realized God had plans for her to be a different kind of "supermodel."

God has a plan for you, too—and it's probably bigger than anything you could ever imagine. In this book you'll begin to reshape the way you see yourself and the way you dream.

Confessions of a Not-So-Supermodel
Faith, Friends, and Festival Queens
Brooklyn Lindsey
RETAIL $9.99
ISBN 978-0-310-27753-8